The World Needs More Love

A Manifesto on Staying in Love with Life
by Y'AKOTO

To my parents and everybody I love.

Cover Artwork by AFROSCOPE

Introduction

I'll never forget the look on my therapist's face.
I think my little horrible story made him uncomfortable. He kept shifting in his expensive chair in his so-called office, which was the ground floor of this massive Victorian mansion.
He probably had the upper floors to himself. The kids were out of the house, and his wife was perhaps grumpy and uninterested in him.
Like so often, I felt slightly out of place but perfectly present in this movie called My Life. He put his chin in his hand and crossed the other arm across his body. After a pause that felt very long, he said, "What are you hoping to change here?"
I looked him straight in the eyes and said:
"All these things mean nothing to me. The fame, the money, the recognition. Fuck that. I want to be able to enjoy life. You know, when you love the little things."

I had written a song about it, called Diamonds. People loved it, especially when I was performing it live. I could see the relief in their faces. It had a positive message that they could all relate to. It's about finding peace of mind, about living freely. I'd like that for myself.

I said it without crying. I felt calm and in control. I couldn't wait to get out of that stuffy space, away from this man who seemed intrigued by me, but also helpless and disoriented. I was dying for a smoke. He annoyed me. His stupid face, stuck in that expression somewhere between pity and unease.

I was 25. Young, yet I felt and looked so old from the inside out. I had achieved quite a lot, yet I was unhappy. Semi-suicidal, even, and not to mention, I was killing it in my career.

"What happened to me... to us... to me and my mother. It haunts me. I can't shake it."

I had recently started burning my wrists with my favorite pink lighter to compensate for the pain. This indescribable, out of nowhere-pain that attacked me most violently when things were going well. Watching my skin burn and deform in front of me was pain I could locate. Pain, I could understand.

Till this day, I have the marks on my left arm. I often thought of getting them done, lasering them, or covering them up with a tattoo, but each time I want to make an appointment, I say to myself: fuck this. This is my story. My skin tells a story. I hurt myself because I got hurt by people who had no business inflicting this outrageous pain on me, as a child.

I didn't mention that to the middle-aged man sitting across from me.
"I'd like to leave now," I said.
I had only been there 30 minutes.

"I'll work with you," I told him, "but it has to be on my terms."
I said it tearlessly.
I didn't know how to cry in front of strangers then.

Watching your mother, your protector, your god, your safe place, get verbally and physically attacked by your father does something to your brain. It rewires you. Nothing adds up when you see that happen. It's the most illogical, nonsensical thing you can experience.
And alongside the happy memories of your childhood, you can't help but acknowledge that you've witnessed something a child should never have seen.

He was supposed to love us. She was supposed to protect me from him. They were both supposed to protect me.
Instead, I learned to protect myself. I've done well in doing that. I can't help but ask myself what would have happened if I had repeated the cycle of toxicity in my family.

Forgiving my parents played a significant role in expanding my being. When you are capable of pure love, you forgive quite easily. I feel pure love for my parents. That unconditional love only a child can feel for their first sensation of a tribe.

Family is our first concept of a true community. That's where we learn everything about life and interaction with other humans. It's our blueprint and our Home.

Everything I have been through has informed me about who I am today. I care deeply for others and how they feel. Because I think it's essential to look out for each other's well-being, regardless of whether it's your family or not.

Through my music, I always felt I could share some of my love with the world. Music has always made me feel better in stressful situations as a child and young adult.

I'm happy that I can do the same for people.

That's where it started. This drive to find out who I am beyond this experience.

Well, I made it out. I broke out of the cycle and am determined to make the best of every day I have left. Not in a weird, fake-positive, forced way, but like, "Yeah, I've been through some stuff, but we made it." Our struggle does not define us.

I'm the sorceress of my reality. I've cultivated transforming every piece of this fragmented childhood into magic. I've spent a fortune, both emotionally and financially, building a safe, honest, and authentic life.

I always knew survival mode wasn't the goal, and I refused to see the world through the lens of trauma, even if I was shaped by it.

What else is out there?

I was sure there was more to gain out of this life. I'm not done believing, loving, and feeling my way through the world. Because the world needs more love, it needs more people connected to their hearts and intuitions, the further we reach the age of digitalism.

In my twenties, I had what people dream of.

I was young and successful, traveling the world with my music: free clothes, five-star hotels, money, and attention. People knew my name. I was supposed to be living the dream.

This period of my life felt so odd to me.

Some days, the waking world seemed like a living hell, and I had to make it through the day without losing my mind.
I did lose it occasionally.

I relentlessly believed in myself and my birthright to be happy and healthy.
I believed in transforming chaos into magic. In writing my own story. In taking back what's mine. In sharing my truth, even if it felt uncomfortable.
Music can do that.
At least I'm convinced it should do that.

Life is fragile and mystical. As much as you can experience it through the veil of your perspective, there is so much to learn about what we all have in common.
The feeling of wanting to be heard, loved, and nourished.
Of feeling joy and ease.
Of being healthy and strong.
Of owning our power and living our lives authentically.

This is what we are about to uncover.

This book isn't about rules or a how-to guide to level up or heal your inner child. I don't believe anyone can tell you how to live your life or heal yourself, and if they do, don't believe them. They don't speak your language. They didn't go through what you went through.

I believe in communication and community.
So here you have it.
My attempt to communicate my life hacks to my community and friends.
To you.

I will reveal a collection of little things I've learned, and unlearned, from falling, getting up, and occasionally doing the most.
So, tell a friend to tell a friend before we dive in.
Some of these chapters might be better shared, argued over, or gossiped about in a voice note.

But whether you read this in one night or one year, I hope it gives you something to hold onto.
Something that feels honest and real.

Now go.
Be weird.
Be different.
Be alive.
Be all of it.

Much love, and welcome to my world.
You will love it here.

Chapter 1
Who the Fuck Does She Think She Is?

I've been called different, crazy, intense, and polarizing by people who made up their minds after meeting me once. I didn't really know what to do with that information, so I didn't pay attention. I filed it under "not my problem" and moved on. My brain was too busy making things, chasing ideas, figuring out how to move out, and dodging my parents' dreams of me becoming something solid, like a doctor, a lawyer, or maybe a teacher if I wanted to be "creative." I didn't have the luxury of overthinking what people said, and I still don't. Honestly, I enjoy the occasional rumor. It's cute and suitable for the field I'm in. All I ever wanted was to live on my terms and do what made sense to me. One of those things, predictably, was being a full-blown artist. In my case, I did not have to become an artist; I already was one. My incredible imagination made me do and see things differently from all my little kindergarten friends. I never liked their games and always invented games that I thought were more fun. I made everybody in my kindergarten class do a towel dance once. I instructed all the kids to get the towels from the bathroom and dance around with them, pretending we were disco angels.

From a very early age, I noticed that certain sounds made my whole body react. I felt the frequency, vibrations, and harmonies like a rush of blood to the head. A beautiful painting could stop time. The ocean made everything make sense, and forests, too. Nothing beats the beauty of our planet Earth. To this day, nature is still the best artist I know and probably the best producer. The moment the wind, waves, and bird-songs merge? Excuse me. Bliss. I wasn't just drawn to music. Anything beautiful pulled me in. If it shimmered, glowed, or had texture, I needed to touch it, stare at it, become it. Eventually, I had to create it. That kind of obsession, let's call it "high-functioning curiosity," shaped me into who I am now: someone who's almost ticked off every dream on her list; I said almost, and keeps building sandcastles and alternate timelines that somehow turn into "reality."

Why "reality" in quotes? Because it's up for debate. Always has been. I figured that out at five years old, when I made my Barbies fly to space in a pink toy car, cooked imaginary plant meals in the garden, and pushed seven cats around in a stroller while announcing myself as their mother to the entire neighborhood. It's not exactly normal, but it's very on brand. Other kids and parents often could not make sense of my spellbound fantasy. I haven't made it to space yet, but I've done things I never thought were possible. And I say that based on my personal scale of what's possible, considering where I started and how often I nearly didn't make it in the 'real' world.

As a child, not older than six, the wall in my room was too white for my taste, so I suggested to my mum that we decorate it. At the time, two things played a vital role in my life: Minnie Mouse and the universe. I loved Minnie Mouse, her positivity, and her two big ears. I would look at my Minnie Mouse doll and think how amazing it must be to hear everything, never to miss a single sound. I loved how she dressed and always seemed ready to have fun. The universe, with its endless stars, galaxies, solar systems, and the fact that nobody really understood it, fascinated me to the point that I would lie awake at night asking myself existential questions. Why are we here? How many children exist on this planet? Are there any children on Pluto? If the galaxy is made of stars, what are we? I remember starting to pray during those moments, because the vastness of it all completely blasted my still-developing child brain. I had full-blown conversations with God about how sad I would be if an asteroid hit us.

My mum agreed to the makeover. We painted Minnie Mouse holding a red balloon next to my bed, and my three favorite planets next to my little keyboard. Whenever I sat in my music corner, I would stare at my universe and feel thoroughly convinced that there was more to discover. Even at that age, I believed everything was possible in my creative process. I would write simple songs about cats, flowers, princesses, and pink cars. Nothing I wrote showed coherence, and that was the beauty of it. School got on my last nerves. Everything had to be done in a particular order, which didn't allow me to think correctly. I recorded everything on my little green cassette player and played my recordings back to myself before I went to bed every night. All my creative output was coated in extreme versatility, playfulness, and range. To this day, I firmly believe my childhood was the ultimate foundation of my artistic brain. Being an only child helped. I could play and exist in my world without being overly interrupted.

Fast forward to my twenties, there were days I didn't want to be here. Days when the grief and the weight of everything made disappearing seem like a reasonable option. But I didn't. Somehow, I stayed.

People still call me "crazy," "complex," "intense," and most consistently, "different." I agree. Being a little unhinged helps, especially if you plan to stay alive and make art.

I learned early that people are quick to call you crazy when you believe in something that isn't "real" yet. When you seem high without actually being on anything, I should have started taking drugs. People thought I was on them anyway. People think you are weird when you hold your ground, the second someone crosses a line. When you somehow become the center of attention just by sitting still and saying nothing. In my case, that was inevitable. I often found myself in situations where I was the "only" one in the room: the only woman, the only writer, the only black woman, the only storyteller, the only one with curls, the only one with a push-up bra and a pack of Marlboro Lights stuck in her cleavage. When I was still smoking, I felt it was convenient to have a cig in your cleavage. I don't smoke anymore. What's the point? It's just nasty. It was my pure presence that got some people on edge. Teachers wrote in my school reports that I was willingly distracting the boys. Was I? Or did these old pervs feel a little turned on by me? I don't know. I didn't think about it further. What I did know was that some of my teachers back then were notoriously known for starting affairs with young students. My class teacher at the time was even married to a former student. That, on the other hand, was wild to me. Who was distracting whom?

When you're not afraid to feel what you feel or to let life be precisely what it is, while still having fun, knowing that this existence can be light, dark, confusing, or gorgeous, some people might call you arrogant. That very acceptance of how things were at the time, without letting myself down, made people think I was overly confident for my age. People will call you difficult when you're not scared of confrontation, especially when protecting your boundaries.

One of my exes was the first to call me a witch. I was 27. I dismissed it immediately. I wasn't a witch, I was just a girl trying to survive the circus of being alive. But I think there are many ways to get 'othered' as a woman. One way of doing that is by labeling women witches. I was also going through phases where I just wanted to be normal, relatable. I thought maybe if I played along, life would be easier. So I ran a little experiment in blending in. When the people around me acted insecure, I mirrored it. When they downplayed themselves, I followed suit. If someone complimented me, I brushed it off to keep things neutral, bland, and manageable.

It worked. Everyone felt comfortable, I had more friends, and people wanted to be around me more. They loved the new me. I was obtainable, a category they understood, a box they could label. I felt dead inside. I've tried my hardest to be normal my whole life, but it doesn't work. I admire conformity and structure. There is something beautiful about being square and just like everyone else. I just physically can't do it. Like, I try, but it never worked for me. I had to become who I am. Nothing felt more artificial than pretending to live a life, like a glove that didn't fit me, or worse, a life that quietly disrespected the core belief that has always kept me sane: anything you can imagine is possible if you dare to be yourself. Authenticity, to me, was always the "now" disguised in the "future."

Maybe I was a little witch, a term often used derogatorily to label women as evil, conniving, and dangerous. I was intrigued.

It kept happening. People kept calling me a witch, sometimes completely unprovoked. I could be in the club dancing, and a guy would talk to me about my "witchy" eyes. He was a cutie for saying that. I would be in the kitchen, refusing to use certain ingredients because I was sure they were poisonous, and my friends would say, 'Alright, Queen Kitchen Witch.' I'd disappear in the forest by myself for hours, humming melodies and looking at trees, and when I came back, my then-roommate would say, Oh, did you have fun doing your witchy things? I would listen to my intuition and tell a friend that the guy she dated didn't love her. She hated me in the moment and came up with an excuse for why she had to leave immediately. A few days later, she would find out he had cheated or done something. My friends would then call just to start the two-hour convo with: you fucking witch!

Back in the present, I picked up this theme in my work and named my fourth album Part 4: The Witch. With all that, I decided to look into the history of witches. Research, obviously.

The history of witches is basically a highlight reel of what happens when women (and some men) dare to think for themselves. The moment you didn't behave, blend in, or shut up you were suspicious. Different? Witch. Unmarried? Witch. Childless? Witch. Unruly? Witch. Did you know how to mix herbs? Ask questions? Know a lot about childbirth? A witch. The whole thing was less about spells and magic and more about control. Witch hunts were never really about witches; they were about power. The church, the state, and everyone benefiting from the status quo needed to keep free thinkers and members of societies who didn't quite conform in check, especially the female ones.

And still, these people dared to live differently, to offer ideas, create medicine, protect their communities, trust their intuition, and, God forbid, exist outside the system. That kind of courage? Terrifying. So terrifying, that up to 60,000 women, men, and children were tortured and killed, all in the name of keeping things "safe and traditional." It's sickening, but also telling.

You don't burn people unless you're terrified of what they know. Very interesting.

As someone who is mixed race, I've always felt like proof of contradiction, a walking question mark in a world addicted to clear labels. I never chose or picked sides. Society views me as a Black woman. That's cool. Still, I remain white, too. I'm both simultaneously thinking, breathing, and existing in both worlds, merging them through my existence. I understand why people can't relate to that. It's a lot to compute, especially when you confidently refuse to pick sides while holding both sides accountable.

In some parts of the world, no one cares. That is why I have chosen London as my home. New York also gave me that feeling of complete oblivion regarding my identity, which was very refreshing. It would be great to live there one day, and I probably will.

In other parts of the world, being mixed already sets you apart socially and historically. You're a reminder of something unresolved, a visible outcome of a system that tried to rewrite origin stories, erase culture, and interrupt lineage. You don't fit inside borders because those borders were never designed for you. Your existence is proof of that.

The transatlantic slave trade wasn't just a crime. In my opinion, it was an act of terror. It was an interruption of families, futures, entire civilizations, and human evolution itself. Colonialism didn't just extract gold, bodies, and land. It extracted memory, language, pride, and rhythm. It left people divided from each other, their ancestors, and themselves.

I've spent large parts of my life on two very different continents, Europe and Africa, and I've seen the aftermath with my own eyes. Africa is still trying to remember itself while reshaping its identity in the present. Europe still suffers from amnesia, shouting into the abyss: Can we just let the past be the past? Nations on both sides are scrambling to reconstruct what was shattered over centuries. It will take generations to begin restoring balance.

This confusion shows up everywhere, even in how people engage with me. Some people I meet need to define what I am, label me, and soften their discomfort by slotting me into something familiar. But I don't belong to a binary. I won't choose a side. I'm both; I embody both opposing races and created my own. That's the only honest position I can take for now. And while all of this continues, the searching, the sorting, the categorizing, we're still waging wars, exploiting countries, destroying ecosystems, and isolating entire groups of people: witch hunts, manhunts, different names, same story. Division is still a powerful tool that we need to start decoding if we want to survive as a species, unless an asteroid takes us out.

Well... humans live in the world they've built inside themselves. The pain we avoid becomes the violence we inflict. We project our inner chaos outward and call it normal. We say we're evolving, but mostly, we're stuck in rotation, forward and backward, aggressively and progressively. Nothing has really changed, and yet, everything keeps changing.

Life isn't fair. The universe doesn't care about your five-year plan, star sign, or vision board. Suppose you call yourself a witch, magician, artist, or not. It will do what it does. We're just here for a bit, our short life ahead of us, trying not to lose our minds while pretending we've got it together. The Earth will continue to turn, with or without our approval. One day, we'll die. Our movie wraps up, our singular consciousness ends, the credits roll, and people will cry into their champagne glasses and gossip about the canapés at your wake.

So yes, there's urgency, not panic, but clarity. We need to live loudly on our terms, one beautiful breath at a time. I won't tell you to be more mindful or eat gluten-free. I don't have the answers to anything, but I can offer some ease, laughter, storytelling, unconventional advice, and companionship on the way.

The more I explored, the more I realized that being an artist isn't about writing songs, performing them, or ensuring you reach as many people as possible with your work. It's about staying connected to what's real. Your reality. And what's real? Everything you feel. Contrast. Chaos. Beauty. Joy, grief, anger, light, and dark all stacked next to each other like mismatched furniture in a house that somehow still feels like home.

Life is confusing. Messy. Occasionally brilliant. I choose to stay here in the moment with you. You don't need to be perfect, just honest. You're allowed to be a masterpiece and a mess. You can cry in the shower and dance in front of your mirror five minutes later. You can change your mind, start again, and then start again… again. That is the path.

So who cares what people say? Who cares what you even think about yourself? You are here to exist. That's your only job. That's your only purpose.

People will have many things to say about anyone who chooses themselves over the perception others have of them. The world needs more love, and we both know what that means. We need to start with ourselves and spread ourselves thick onto everything we touch and everyone we come into contact with. Love is truly the only way to heal the world and make it a better place.

Being in control of your own story is the first thing I recommend, because it determines the outcome of your life. What do you want? How do you want to see yourself? How far are you willing to go to fulfill your imagination of your world? If you can imagine it, it's already there. It already exists. Now we have to get the body to follow suit. How are you feeling today? What do you need?

The world needs more people who dare to be who they truly are without shrinking, performing, or seeking permission.

Chapter 2
Why You Should Stop Trying Immediately

Why do we keep trying and then try to make ourselves feel better for just... trying? Why do we give up quickly when things get sticky, challenging, or emotionally overwhelming? Are we okay? Is this normal? Why do some of us have such little belief in ourselves? The world needs more people who believe in their ability to do things they love.

I used to get so frustrated when songs stayed unfinished in the studio. It felt like I had deceived myself. How much did I believe in my ability to create music? My producers would say, "You can get back to it tomorrow," and I'd say, "No. Why? To let my ideas go sour like the milk I never drink because it bloats me like a hot air balloon on its way to space?" There was magic in finishing those sessions, even just leaving with a demo, something I (and others) could build on, felt like a win, a little proof of belief, a spark that stayed lit. It might not have been the perfect song, but it was the result of my self-respect.

Every studio session counts. My attempt to create something mattered, even with all the challenges it brought up. And yes, I always came back to it the next day. But at least I had a finished song that just needed polishing. I told myself that the future is always created in the moment, and that I'm not in the business of wasting time, energy, and life force. I'm not bringing this up because I'm an expert in completing tasks, but rather a lifelong student, and I'd like to share my research with you.

You've probably heard it: "I'm trying to be an artist," "I'm trying to be a better parent," "I'm trying to change my diet," "I'm trying to make more money," blah blah blah. Trying isn't doing, and it's time to step fully into what we want without hesitation. I was always a songwriter in my mind, and it was never my intention to "try" and be one. Even as a little girl, just five years old, my poetic enthusiasm was underlined, writing poems like: A fat cat sat on a mat: the end.

Trying and not completing something is like a soft pillow giving you a bad neck every morning. It feels like movement and progress, but nothing changes. It gives you the illusion of progress without the risk of failure. It's a self-soothing sedative dressed up as ambition. Yes, yes, at least you tried.

I decided this for myself: trying isn't doing, and nobody hands out cookies for good intentions. You are not a toddler. "I'm trying" is code for "I haven't committed yet." It's also the anthem of people who want to seem humble, safe, digestible. But shrinking yourself doesn't make the world more generous. It just makes you forgettable.

Have you ever argued with someone about a repetitive pattern of things that upset you, and they keep saying: But I'm trying. Are they? Or is it like in one of my songs? "Fool me once, shame on you; fool me twice, shame on me too." How many chances do we give ourselves before we take action, get prepared, and get shit done? Doing means creating electricity. It's the full inhale and the full exhale.

It's when your body moves before your mind catches up. It's messy, uncertain, and real. It feels good to complete a mission over and over again. People can feel the difference. They know when you're dabbling. They know when your energy is stuck in the performative limbo of trying too hard. That vibe? It's repellent. It says, "I'm not sure I belong here." They can smell your hesitance, self-doubt, or even worse, your inability to focus and keep your word.

But the air changes the second you step into doing, fully, unapologetically. You stop asking for permission. You stop explaining yourself. You stop auditioning for your own allowance to live and explore your own power. Whether it's love, work, health, or art, you're doing it the minute you decide, even if it's awkward. Even if you fail, especially if you fail. Failing is sexy. It proves that you are unafraid and makes you interesting enough for people to relate to you.

The concept of trial and error is overrated. When you're in it, actually in it, failure isn't a verdict. It's scenery. The error becomes the glitch and self-empowerment mantra that will catapult you to your next level. Not "the" level but YOUR level. Because your next level is not my next level. Period. You move through it like the self-appointed badass you are.

Here's your experiment: Delete "trying" from your vocabulary for one week. Watch how fast your energy shifts. Watch how the people around you start treating you differently. You don't have to fake confidence. Just commit, quietly, firmly, casually, like it's already yours.

Whenever I envision a studio session, I set myself a goal. I'm completing at least three songs. Everybody's time is precious and limited, including mine. When you listen to my songs, many of them speak about how short life is and how this time spent here on this planet sometimes feels more like an interval between life and death. In "Body Movement," I speak about that. In "We Walk the Line," I clarify that we will always be losers and winners, regardless of where we stand in life.

This is how you trick your brain into brilliance, not by effort but embodiment. Your brain does not know the difference between attempting to do something and actually doing it.

So, why should you stop trying immediately? Because your life deserves more than hesitant maybes and half-finished dreams. The world needs more people who believe in what they do. Let's go. You've got this. Your brain doesn't know the difference between imagining and doing. So, show it who's in charge.

The world needs more people who trust the truth of what they feel and believe in what they can build, even before it's fully formed.

Chapter 3
Be Angry

Anger is underrated. It's one of the most intelligent emotions we have. It shows up like the defense shield of your body. Loud, dramatic, slightly inconvenient, but always right on time to make things right for yourself. Knowing when something's off before your brain has caught up. It's not always graceful and rational, but it's honest. Several things make me angry. Anger always comes before sadness. It's the emotion I feel before I can even reach true grief. It's what shows up when I feel purposefully misunderstood, see someone being treated unfairly, or remember my parents fighting over things I didn't understand as a little girl. How painful it must have been to constantly live in a battle zone.

It comes up in work too, when you know you're being taken advantage of, when someone who's already made up their mind about you speaks with judgment and says things designed to hurt you. Intentionally. Standing up for myself as a songwriter and composer is where I learned one of the most important lessons of my life: always argue your case.

And surround yourself with people who make it their business to speak up for you. Too many times I've seen people humbled into being "the bigger person." Told to let it go. Be gracious. Don't cause a scene.

Especially women are being fed that deadbeat narrative. Maybe so boys and men can beautifully immerse themselves into being the emotional, irrational divas that they sometimes are, always disguising it under manhood and masculinity? No, thank you.

There was no way anyone would fake-humble me out of my writing credits when I knew exactly what I brought to the table. That made me a target early on in my career. Oh, excuse me, it is not my kink to give in just to avoid confrontation with people who expect me to perform oral sex on them. Some producers were beautiful people with utmost respect for my craft and presence. Others made moves on me. Thinking back now, I should have ratted them out to my label or manager. But deep down, I probably knew that no one would listen or take me seriously. The music industry is sexist. That's the answer I mostly got when I questioned some individuals' despicable behavior. In my personal life, I made it very clear that I was not to be fucked with. What came out of my traumatic experiences as a child was a certain discernment that worked every single time.

I once threw a man out onto the street because he told me, to my face, that I smelled like ass. In my own house, if I must add. Don't ask me why he said it. I'm still not entirely sure. But I'm pretty confident it was a calculated attempt to hurt me and make me feel disgusting. And, plot twist, he admitted that later, because I was naïve enough to think closure was something I needed. I threw him out in the middle of the night, hooked up with him a couple of times because I lacked boundaries, and then started hitting on his best friend. Now that really got the ball rolling. I didn't care. Anger got me to toy around with his emotions for a bit because it felt appropriate. This is what happens when you believe he's different. When you tell yourself he won't be intimidated by your early success or your financial independence. When you think he's evolved enough not to feel threatened by a woman who doesn't need him to pay her rent. He wasn't different. He just waited a little longer to show it.

Ever felt that blood-boiling sensation? That moment when you can't swallow your spit and your heart starts pumping. Like your mind's full of explosions and you're the only one hearing them? That's anger. It appears for various reasons, including injustice, rudeness, past trauma, betrayal, or simply someone being an idiot in traffic. Life is unfair. Expecting it not to be is setting yourself up for uncontrollable delusion. I'm not here to tell you to count to ten and breathe. I do it sometimes, but I'm skeptical. I'm against the notion of mindfulness when it suppresses your emotions.

I'm here to tell you: Let that shit out.

You need to make space for the rage to leave your body. Your health, physical, emotional, and spiritual, depends on it. Holding onto anger, or worse, letting it rot into self-hate, will eat you alive. We've all had those nights when we can't sleep because we didn't speak up. Replaying a scene, thinking, damn, I should've told that person to fuck off. And science agrees: bottling anger leads to stress, heart problems, burnout, and a weakened immune system. Nothing is worth that. Your body is your home; stop letting people set fires in it. To the ones who pride themselves on being "above it, " are you calm or numb? If you are all balanced and perfectly calm. Congrats. Stop judging others who are not.

Here's what has helped me in my experience.

Move. Go for a walk. Jump around. Dance. Lift something heavy. Movement pulls you out of the story in your head and puts you back in your body, where your power lives. The amount of power I felt within me when I started lifting weights was incredible.

Confront. Ask people what they meant. If something felt like a dig, call it out. You're not confrontational. You're awake. Personally, I prefer direct confrontation. If you're the one who triggered me, you should feel some of the heat. That's not vengeance; instead, it could be referred to as balance. I'm not swallowing poison just to protect someone else's comfort.

Create. Make something, music, art, a long letter you never send, channel it. That kind of release is clean, useful, and underrated. Creating anything has always helped improve my mood and life. Scream. In a bathroom, in your car, into a pillow. Whatever works. A loud, ugly scream is worth a lot. I'm a big fan. Sometimes you need to train your vocals. What better way to be and feel heard? Laugh like a crazy sad clown. It confuses your nervous system in a good way. Changes the expression in your face and signals the mind that you are above this shit without being run over by it.

I don't care how you deal with it as long as you dare to confront it in its entirety.

Overthinking won't save you. Writing might. Movement definitely will. Anger is not your enemy.

You do not have to keep calm at all times. It's your alarm system. It's the part of you that still believes you deserve better. If we want the world to feel more love, we need to give ourselves permission to feel our anger, too. Real love can't grow in emotional denial.

The world needs more people who can feel anger without turning it into harm, who can let it rise, move through them, and still choose clarity over chaos.

Chapter 4
You Are a Liar, and That's Okay

We all say we prefer the truth, until it's the one truth we don't want to hear. The one that lights our ego on fire. We're still the kings and queens of denial. Always have been. "The truth sets you free" only sounds good when someone hot and mysterious says it in a black and white movie while you sob into your wine glass. I had to face my truth when I saw myself on TV for the first time. Awkward. Shy. Foreign. I was sitting next to real celebrities, chefs, actors, and politicians, pretending to know what I was doing. Meanwhile, the host had no mercy, drilling me with banal, superficial questions, and there I was: all eyes on me, giant cameras capturing every uncomfortable second. I had just gotten signed to Warner Music Europe, and this was supposed to be a big slot. Not even sure if I understood what that meant. My parents never took my attempts to become an artist seriously. I even felt a consistent notion of resentment from my mother once it was clear that I was following an artistic path. She was working in different countries all over the world, and my father and I had a type of on-and-off relationship.

I hated sitting at that show. Was that really me? Did I realize this was one of the biggest opportunities of my life? One of the most-watched shows on prime time television? Apparently not. The casting director even called my management to complain about my "standoffish behavior." I was 22, allergic to small talk, and completely unequipped to be a show pony. They wanted my energy and sparkle. Instead, I gave them existential dread. He was right. That was weird of me, but that was all I could offer at the time.

For the first time, I was judged by the world. Some people loved my awkwardness on TV, some hated it. I never read YouTube comments. But that's when I was confronted with the fact that people tell you their truth even if you didn't ask for it. It's fine, I thought. I was not going to hate myself for messing this up. My truth is the most powerful of all. I forgave myself quickly for not getting it right, and that was all that mattered.

The truth always lies within someone's individual perception. My truth is not your truth, and vice versa. We all perceive so-called "facts" from different realities. I know it's the most generic thing to say, but the truth is often generic. We're taught that honesty is our North Star, only to discover a world tangled in a web of complex problems: wars, environmental issues, social challenges, global health crises, and big corporations constantly trying to sell "the truth" to us. In summary, what "feels" true to you is true to you. How funny is that? If anything, being completely truthful is often conceived as a misplaced virtue, sometimes even seen as weak. People experience alienation for uncovering uncomfortable truths or being praised as heroes, depending on how lucky they get. How complicated is that? I was often scolded for saying what's on my mind, whether it was in school, with my parents, or in my job. I just don't have anything to hide. Never did.

It's not shocking that every now and then, scandals break out involving people who have sold the idea of truth to us. I call them "The how to people," how to be richer, happier, healthier, blah blah blah. Shut the heck up. Regularly, they are exposed for being the complete opposite. Abusing their spouse, committing tax fraud, and drinking children's blood. I'm joking. Lighten up, I'm trying to make a point. You get it, right?

The only person you should never lie to is yourself. Strategize your truths, save the unfiltered versions for the mirror. The fear of society's raised eyebrows and judgments makes some people disguise their authentic selves and drown themselves in pretense. If you suppress something that reflects your desires, you will most likely become unhappy. Life's charm lies in its unpredictability, like a kaleidoscope of perspectives on truth. That's what makes the world go round. Let people be. Let's judge less and turn the mirror to ourselves. Controversial confession: I've lightened my grip on truth's pursuit. It's a rabbit hole, and if you're not careful, you might end up with truth-induced depression. Ever gone truth hunting and found more confusion than clarity? Welcome to the club. Sometimes I just remain oblivious on purpose.

Be strategic about the truth. Not everyone deserves to know the truth. Ask yourself whether you can live with the repercussions of telling a lie. How good or bad are your lies? Distinguish between helpful lies and unhelpful lies. We are all delusional. Don't let anyone make you feel like they are the morality police of truth. Let's be clear. Ask your conscience. If you want to sleep in peace, I suggest not lying about things that involve human life, death, abuse, or betrayal. Covering this up will be stressful and will most likely come to light. What's in the dark must come to light. Lie about your resume to get the job you want? Hell yes. Lie about whether you dated that embarrassing ex. Absolutely. Tell someone they look gorgeous, even though they don't, just to get something out of them? By all means.

Let's not kid ourselves. We live in a world where even the most virtuous curate their image. Strategic lying and truth-bending are the only way forward. Feel it and believe it. Your brain doesn't know the difference between illusion and reality. Tell yourself you've already made it. Truth be told, no one knows if you really have, as long as they believe it, it's true. Create, disguise, and pretend. We all do. I did it after I messed up that show. I just kept going and brushed it off. After all, this was the beginning of my career. There were so many more errors and failures to come. I was not going to be intimidated by getting this stuffy TV show wrong.

The world may need more truth, but authentic self-love begins when we dare to be honest with ourselves first.

Chapter 5
Family Over Everything but Yourself

Some people get nervous before speaking publicly or going on stage. I get nervous at family gatherings, even though I'm not close to any family members except my mother. Family gatherings are the creepiest, most stressful thing to me. Even with all the therapy I have had, I take deep breaths before heading to a family event, whether it's my own or someone else's family.

A friend once asked me, "Can you summarize your life story in four minutes?" I wouldn't even be able to fit my toddler years into four minutes. If you want to know my life story, I've shared it in numerous articles, Wikipedia entries, and interviews. However, I found her exercise very interesting. Your destiny speaks for itself. I don't like to generalize, but our life experiences shape us, depending on our origins and the conditioning we receive. I told her I couldn't do it. Come on, she said. I said no. It won't work.

I've often had to explain where I feel most at home: Ghana or Germany. The audacity of being both leaves many people second-guessing which culture I most identify with, none of them. I've created my interpretation of it. It's a unique identity and cultural heritage that does not fit the categories of being German or Ghanaian. The first place I ever truly felt at home was London, a city that had nothing to do with my identity yet embraced me without asking where I was from. I had lived in Paris for a while. But that was different. As much as I loved living in Paris, it did not feel like home. London did. Perhaps it was the fact that everyone spoke English, the language I grew up with, or the similarities to Ghanaian culture, which makes sense when you consider that Ghana was a former British colony. I also had that coming-home feeling when I walked through New York for the first time. It was a cold March day and I wore my infamous fake fur purple coat. I got it two sizes up to look oversized and huge. This lady yelled from the other side of the road. "You better work, girl, that coat is fire." She was beautiful and loud, straight-striding cat walking, not missing a single beat. I yelled, thank you babe and gave her my biggest smile. I'd never felt more at home in my life.

Life is challenging in really big cities. Everything is expensive, and just like New Yorkers, Londoners don't waste time tracing your bloodline when they first meet you. The city does not wait for you to figure it out. Everyone works so hard and has to give their ultimate best. We keep it moving with an extraordinary pace that allows you to find out more about yourself than others because there's simply no time to look over your shoulder and compare yourself to others.

My mother was born and raised in the north of Germany. My father spent his life growing up in the east of Ghana, and later travelled through Europe with his music, where he met my mother. They fell in love instantly, and after three years, I was born. My father, a trained engineer, activist, artist, and musician, wanted to move to Ghana with my mother and me, a trained social educator. She loved books, was a passionate traveler, and inspired parents in organized groups to parent creatively while considering their children's cultural backgrounds. They shared one vision: to raise me in Ghana and have me grow up bilingual. The aim was to move naturally between Europe and Africa. My father was keen on letting me know where I was from and raising me in his home country. Till this day, I am forever grateful to him for his conviction and pride. He was right about raising me in both places equally.

Throughout our time in Ghana, my mother spoke to me in both German and English, while my father addressed me in English. He said he wasn't interested in me learning the local languages because they wouldn't help me thrive internationally. He was right. I went on to write all my songs in English, participate in writing camps worldwide, and am now writing my first self-published book in English. I still make a considerable effort to express myself in Twi. It is still one of my aims to speak it fluently one day.

My parents made it work. Neither of them comes from money. My mother was the first in her family to attend university, and my father was the first in his to travel overseas. They were both cycle breakers in their unique way, and I respect them immensely for that.

In Ghana, my mother worked as a secretary and later as a teacher, while my father continued to pursue his music career.

My childhood in Ghana taught me to believe in my ability to express myself. For the longest time, I was the only mixed-race kid in class until I met James. He was my little friend. He was a handsome boy whose mother was a white English lady and whose father was a Ghanaian military man. He was my fierce protector. From that point on, we rolled together. He used to stand up for me in front of the other kids. I was an easy target. I stood out, my hair looked wild and untamed compared to the other girls with their perfect, neat cornrows. I was shy but also an extrovert in a strange commanding way. He gave me occasional gifts, mostly colorful, oversized children's books. Some of them told the classic stories of Red Riding Hood or Rapunzel. I was obsessed with these gifts. They were almost always brand new. I often wondered what he told his parents when they asked where all his storybooks had gone. Did he tell his mum he gave them to me straight away? Or did he make up stories about losing them? I will never know. He was very kind to me. And I was thankful to have him by my side in a school where we were constantly reminded that we didn't belong. I wonder where he is now, because I want to let him know that he made coming to school every morning ten times easier.

I was eleven when my parents' money started to run out, and they decided to head back to Germany. My mother and I went first. When I was standing at Kotoka Airport and my mother told me to say goodbye to my father, I honestly thought she was joking. I guess I was too young to comprehend that we were leaving for good.

Back in Germany, I was put straight into school and hated it more than anything. I was the only mixed-race kid in class; again, I was the different one. Some loved me for it, others hated me. I will never forget this girl in first grade refusing to share her crayons with me, but then happily passing them over to everyone at our table. I thought she was the meanest girl on earth. She probably still is. I missed my friends in Ghana, and the German teachers looked like big, old, blown-up Father Christmas cartoons without the red outfit. I made two or three friends, became a singer and dancer (mostly in school or sports institutions), and decided that I would never try to fit into any group that already looked at me like I was different.

The theme in my life has always been not to let those who couldn't accept me for who I am define the direction of my path. Even as a child, I grew wary of advice that didn't match the actions or integrity of the person giving it. Good advice doesn't come from a place of judgment. I always knew that.

I never listened to any teacher who told me I wasn't good enough, especially when they made no effort to teach me in a way I could understand. I was bilingual, constantly singled out for not sticking to one language, and already struggling under the weight of bullying and passive aggression from both students and staff. Not one teacher asked how I was doing. Teachers hold the power to make or break a child's spirit. I'm still shocked that anyone can become a teacher just by studying hard enough, with zero psychological evaluation. I saw too many unstable adults in classrooms, always quick to paint me as the villain simply because I refused to shrink for their authority. They rewarded obedience over individuality and had no interest in acknowledging my talent, only focusing on my shortcomings.

At the age of 13, I was the lead singer of a rock, pop-soul band in high school. Don't ask me how it happened. It just did. We played shows everywhere, and we were pretty popular at the time.

I founded a dance class at school because it felt like the right thing to do. I was constantly bored, and school lacked any real creative stimulation, so I had to invent things that were fun and interesting to me. My dance class was one of them. They all came, even the boys. I choreographed a routine to Destiny's Child's "No No No" and before I knew it, the whole school was dancing it. I couldn't wait to graduate and finally get out of that place. It felt so stifling to be there.

My father was in a bad mood. Germany didn't suit him, and he knew that from the beginning. His spirit dimmed when his music career didn't go as planned. The factory jobs he worked in made him depressed. Too many reminders that talent doesn't guarantee dignity. My father was a true artist. Working just to survive or provide made him deeply unhappy.

As a child, I often wished I hadn't been born; my parents were constantly fighting about money and parenting. My dad would yell, "She is your daughter." That hurt. I never felt wanted by my father. I can now contextualize the stress he was going through. But when you are younger, it stings to feel like you are the reason your parents are fighting when it was about how to come up with money to finance the next school trip.

My mother became the leading provider; she had always been, even during our time in Ghana. I never understood why my father was so pained by the fact that she made more money than he did. She loved his music and work. She always supported him. She worked, took care of me, knitted his big, look-defining hats that resembled vinyls and came to his shows. She must have felt so alone and tired of the constant attacks when she was just trying to provide for her family. I got into the habit of turning the music up as high as it would go when they were fighting and singing along to every song that came on.

Destiny's Child. TLC. Brandy. My holy trinity. Oh, and Aaliyah. The queen of my life at the time.

My mother's Family lived in Germany, and I was often dropped off at my aunt's house. She had three kids, and my mum didn't have time for me after school because she was working. So, I had to go to her sister's house frequently. I was the only black girl in that neighborhood, and the cycle of not feeling like I belonged continued. The unthinkable happened at my aunt's house. At about 11 years old, I was sexually molested by one of the older boys. A friend of my cousin's. He was about 6 years older than I was. The boys in his circle were ruthless. There was a trend among our group to grope the girls. They would violently grab your private parts from behind and touch your whole crotch. Sometimes they would even lift you, touching you everywhere. It was so humiliating and painfully degrading. I remember thinking about kicking and fighting back, and sometimes I did. They were all just so much bigger than me.

Between then and my graduation, there was another stop: Yaoundé, Cameroon. I was 14 and thank God my parents had already split. After separating from my dad, my mother completed a university course that allowed her to work in German development services. She immediately signed her first contract, which took us to Cameroon, a beautiful, central African country with complex politics and a stagnant economy.

My father was in a bad mood. Germany wasn't the place for him, even though he'd known that from the start. His spirit broke after his music didn't go as well as he imagined, after being exposed to racism over and over again, working lousy jobs in factories and workshops. In retrospect, I understand his permanently bad mood. After my parents' separation, my mother helped my father find a flat so he could move out. I remember her helping him to renovate it. After everything she had been through with him, after all the verbal and physical attacks. She assisted him in starting over. Love truly speaks volumes. When I ask her why she did that, she says, 'He is your father.' You are my child. He is the father of my child.

While living in Cameroon with my mum for almost two years, I learned French, took more dance classes, played on a basketball team, and wrote more songs. Mostly by myself, late at night, after I had sat for hours writing little thriller stories about female assassins on my PC at the time. I would want to publish them one day.

The American high school my mum sent me to opened a new world. Americans thought everything was "amazing." For the first time, teachers spotted my talent and challenged me in the fields of art.

That's also when I developed my eating disorder.

I remember throwing up every night before my mum got home and going for 7km runs, because sitting still and hearing my thoughts could easily turn into a nightmare. I started drinking and smoking. Never too much. Never too obvious. I loved cigarettes. The hot smoke in my throat. The raspiness in my voice. But I was smart. I never got caught, and nobody questioned me. My mum was busy with her new life and new boyfriend. I hated him: a new man, a new intruder who could potentially go rogue. We left Cameroon when I was 16 years old. We are now back in Germany, and a few years later, I finally graduated.

I could finally leave this bloody institution called school. I needed to get out of there as soon as possible and embark on the journey of living my own independent life. At some point in my early twenties, I told my mum that I didn't want to attend family gatherings anymore. She resisted. But she understood. I was tired of enhancing my PTSD symptoms by sitting in my aunt's house pretending we were one big happy family.

If you've been blessed with a loving, supportive family, hold onto that. Dwell in it. Carry that love with you wherever you go and spread it around like wildfire. People need love. The world needs a lot of love. Very often, we are not receiving it where we are supposed to, in our family. Let's face it: Some of us didn't hit the jackpot in terms of family dynamics. If that's you, this isn't about feeling sorry for yourself; it's about perspective. It's about digging through the dirt to find clarity and comfort in yourself as an individual who can still be part of a family. You always come first. That's the rule.

Family is the first institution we're conditioned by. They're the original influencers, shaping our earliest thoughts, beliefs, and insecurities. They're supposed to guide, nurture, and love us unconditionally, and even if they do, it doesn't mean you owe them the keys to your identity. Don't let anyone talk you into living a life that doesn't feel like yours, not even your own relatives.

Later, when I lived in Paris, I went on my habitual walks, and after an hour, I sat next to an older lady on the bench. I love old French people. They are unhinged and honest, telling you everything that's on their mind, without being asked. I said hello and sat down. She did not even bother to turn to the side and she said: La vie est comme un sablier : une fois que tu meurs, le temps s'arrête. Il ne se passe plus rien. Tu continues juste à vivre dans la mémoire des autres. Life is like an hourglass: once you die, time stops. Nothing happens. You just live on in people's memories. It made me remember how short and meaningless this all gets, considering that you only have this little time to be alive. Mortality can remind us of our vitality in a drastic way. I made it a point to confront anyone and everyone, even if they were part of my own family, when I felt that they took away some of my inner peace. It didn't matter who they were anymore. This was my life, and it is my time on this planet. I give myself full authority and permission to make use of this time however I want.

If you've picked up this book, chances are you're here to challenge the status quo, to peel back the layers of your existence, and maybe even dismantle some of the crap you were raised to believe. Most of our core beliefs are passed down to us from our families. That's not inherently bad, but have you stopped to ask yourself: Do they still serve me? Am I able to serve love to the world while holding on to the pain my family inflicted on me?

It's okay to want something different, or even less than your family expects of you. It's OK to step out of the clan mentality. Every family has that one person who breaks patterns. Maybe it's you. Perhaps you're the one who doesn't fit the script, who refuses to play the role written for them. If so, welcome to the club of aliens who live by their unique definition and desires.

The first ten years of our lives are like an open hard drive. Every word, every action, every trauma gets downloaded and stored. Your parents, whether they meant to or not, left their fingerprints all over your psyche. That's just the reality of growing up.

For me, that download came with a mix of adventure, chaos, domestic violence, emotional abuse, and a constantly shifting environment. I'm not here to unload my life story because oversharing makes me cringe. Yet, here I am because it's almost like I don't care anymore. It's essential I went through this to become the person I am today. Marina Abramović once said, "The more pain and suffering, the better the art." She's not wrong. There's a rawness in people who work through their pain publicly, whether in music, performance, or any creative outlet. But let's not romanticize this. It's unnatural as hell to process your trauma for an audience. The self-destruction you see in artists who burn bright and fast, even so that some of them unfortunately do not survive. That's not a life path. It's a warning. I never understood why pop culture overlooks the fact that most good artists are individuals who have gone through life transforming their experiences into imagery. Or essentially something we can hear, feel, or touch.

Our parents are our source. We come into this world dependent on them, looking to them for everything. And because of that, they can't help but project their fears, failures, and unfulfilled dreams. Some parents push their kids into careers they want for themselves or set impossible standards for relationships and success. Others repeat the trauma they went through, often without even realizing it. Most people, including members of your family, aren't reflecting on how to break cycles; they're too busy surviving their own trauma. Reflection is a luxury, and breaking generational patterns takes work. You must recognize what's being projected onto you and decide if you will continue living life through and for your family. I have forgiven my parents because the world needs more love and peace. Peace that starts from within.

Let's get practical. How do you deal with parents or family without getting dragged back into their web of expectations and unresolved issues? Know your triggers. If specific conversations or situations make you feel sad or angry, identify them and try to avoid them when possible. Set boundaries. You don't have to answer every call. You don't have to attend every family gathering. Communicate honestly. If something hurt you as a kid, speak up. Non-confrontational but honest communication can be a game-changer. You can't fix your parents. You can only fix yourself. Let go of that weight. It's not yours to carry. Sometimes the best thing you can do is step back. Take a breather from toxic family dynamics. Distance doesn't mean you don't care. It means you finally care about yourself. I don't buy into the "blood is thicker than water" nonsense. Loyalty is earned, not owed, even to family. Forgiveness? Sure. I've forgiven people in my family. But forgetting? Never. The moment I stopped trying to mend broken relationships was when my life began to open up. New opportunities, new love, genuine connection. It was like the universe had been waiting for me to cut the cord. I invested in my mental health, and suddenly I could see clearly. You've probably met people who seem like they've got it all together. Trust me, everyone's carrying something. The difference is that some people choose to offload what doesn't serve them. If you're already in the process of cutting those energetic cords, keep going. If you haven't started, leap. It's terrifying. But it's worth it. You don't have to live in someone else's shadow, even if they're your parents or siblings.

Remember this. You didn't come into this world to be a carbon copy of someone else's dreams or regrets. You're here for you. Be loyal to that. Put that above everything. During the editing process of this book, I struggled with this chapter. It feels like the most incoherent one. It lacks context. It's not linear, a literal nightmare. But that's what trauma is. It isn't linear. It isn't a story. It just is. And that's precisely what we need to learn to live with.

The world needs more people who build strong communities rooted in care, love, and kindness. Family can be found wherever there is trust, commitment, and genuine connection.

Chapter 6
Your Friends Are Not the Problem. You Are.

There's nothing nicer than having your house full of friends. People you love. People who make you feel warm and fuzzy inside because they make you laugh, dance, and rejoice. Yes, I'm about to get really tacky talking about how much I personally value friendship. But honestly, it's that intense kind of bond that I think is highly underrated. Friendships can be beautiful, safe havens, placed in a world of their own. I deem good friendships just as meaningful as romantic relationships. One cannot substitute the other. They are both crucial to our mental and physical well-being.

Having a good friend has always kept me sane, grounded, and inspired. In my case, I don't distinguish between men and women. I've had the most intense friendships with both, and I genuinely believe it's an outdated myth that men and women can't just be friends. I'm thankful for every single friend who's been part of my journey. I love the unsolicited advice friends give you. Very entertaining. It was circa 2018 in Paris. Moving to Paris was a significant decision for me. I told a friend, an established musician working globally, that I needed to leave Germany. "It's suffocating," I explained. "I need inspiration. A change. A challenge." He said, "Come to Paris. I have a flat there. You can rent a room." I was thrilled. I took him at his word. I was about 27, touring non-stop, and in desperate need of a change of scenery. I had played every city in Germany and worked in all studios relevant at the time. We made it happen, and next thing you know, we were hanging out the following night in his flat. He wasn't there often. I shared the place with another woman who was also his friend. Occasionally, when he wasn't playing shows and I happened to be home, we'd bump into each other. I loved him, truly, as a friend. There was something fierce and unique about the way he expressed himself. Not only artistically, but also personally. Not the best vocalist, but easily one of the most brilliant lyricists and creative thinkers I've ever come across. One night, I was telling him about the complicated relationship I had with my father, and he said: "Sometimes you just have to respond to madness with madness. The biggest mistake you're making is trying to confront your father with reason. He clearly doesn't understand your calm, intelligent attempt to de-escalate." It was the advice I needed. It came at precisely the right moment, and it changed something in me, even altered my brain chemistry. The next time my father and I had a conflict, I mirrored his behavior. I'd never seen him so shocked. Almost apologetic. It worked.

Sometimes, you just need to ask your friends and try not to get in your feelings when they offer constructive criticism. I no longer talk to that friend, but he changed my life with his advice. Our friendship was perfect timing for where we were in life.

It's beautiful to love your friends. Some of them you've known your whole life. You went to school with them. They helped you out of shitty situations, like my friend did, and some came into your life later and played a significant role in your daily routines or career. All in all, they make you feel better, a support system that outlives breakups, relocations, and age gaps. That's special, important, and vital. Never underestimate that. It's crucial to protect the love we have for our friends. The world needs more healthy support systems outside of work and family.

Ever heard the phrase, "Show me your friends, and I'll tell you who you are"? Yup. We attract our friends based on how we feel about ourselves in certain phases of life. Let's think about it: some of your friends are probably going through things similar to yours right now, and vice versa. Energy is contagious. How we feel, especially about ourselves, is visible and tangible to others, even if we don't talk about it. It's a frequency. It is felt without explanation. We align and connect on a specific frequency. What we give out, we receive. And that's never more obvious than in who we choose to keep around.

Scientists say most friendships are formed in adolescence because that's when we go through a "social reorientation" phase. It's a time when we start rebelling against family and finding our tribe. Your brain develops an area during this time that pushes you out of the nest and into the world. This explains why teenagers are generally more social than kids or adults. Whether it's online or offline, teenagers tend to have more time and desire to socialize. And some might say it's because of the lack of responsibilities they have at an early age. As much as this is true, it is also crucial for them, on both a physical and mental level, to expand their horizons by meeting new people and challenging themselves. I can personally say I've never gotten out of this phase. I love learning about the world through the perception of others. This is tied to something called "Theory of Mind," which is just a fancy way of saying you realize the world doesn't revolve around you. It's about understanding other people's beliefs, feelings, and perspectives. This process takes hold particularly during adolescence, helping us develop empathy and navigate the complex world. Curiosity is essential for expanding your worldview and learning new things.

If you're not an only child like me, you might be thinking, But Yaa, I grew up with my siblings as my best friends. Cool. But that's not a challenge. Those are built-in connections; those are your family. You do not have to challenge yourself to get to know them. You didn't have to go out and create bonds with strangers. Big difference. Creating those connections with strangers helps us maintain an open and flexible mind toward people.

Now, back to friendships. They still play a massive role in our mental development and well-being, regardless of how old we are. We've all felt the emotional wreckage a fight or weird vibe with a friend can cause. But now you're in your late twenties or thirties, and things feel harder. Making new friends or maintaining old ones takes more effort. You might be asking: Why has everyone changed? Why do I get bored with new people so quickly? And then the excuses roll in: I don't have time because of the kids, the job, they are the ones to blame, bla, bla, bla. Friendships have expiry dates. And they should. You can't expect everyone to roll with you forever. People change, and most importantly, you change. Not everybody likes the way you changed, and that's okay. They live in another city, don't have kids, while you do, or vice versa. Life happens. Accept it and develop some healthy detachment. Let them be. Let yourself be. Be patient and focus on making new connections. It's wonderful, trust me. If your friendships feel solid and effortless, with no drama or confusion, skip this chapter. Truly, enjoy it. But if life is shifting, and your so-called friends feel off, distant, or no longer aligned with your energy, listen up: it's not that deep. Move on quietly, cleanly, and without drama. You don't owe anyone theatrics. Let things fade away or come to a peaceful end. It's always to your advantage. Friendship dynamics evolve. The girl you once spoke to daily about boys might now be your go-to for business advice. The one you once saw every weekend may be dealing with something you know nothing about. That guy from school? He's in a new relationship. Your childhood best friend is starting a company and doesn't respond to texts as quickly. You get the picture.

It's not personal. And if it is, who cares? Get over yourself and go do something kind for your nervous system. Take a bath or go for a walk.

Fighting with friends in your thirties (and honestly, even in your twenties) wastes time. If communication breaks down, it's okay to walk away. If things go cold, let them. Not everything needs closure or commentary. Let space do what space does.

We all make mistakes in friendships. We miss calls, overreact, disappear, and return. Accountability matters, but so does letting go. Enjoy your friendships while they're good and stop complaining when they shift. Grow up and make room for what's next.

And if you're bored? That's on you. You're not meeting new people or putting yourself in new environments. Start a class. Go to a concert. Speak to someone at the bar. And no, your partner doesn't count. They are not a replacement for friendship.

Loneliness isn't solved by expecting one person to meet every emotional need. Go outside. Apply the theory of mind. Be around people who challenge your perspective.

Friendship is not passive. It's not just history or shared space, it's a choice you keep making. It takes attention, care, and showing up when it's inconvenient.

It's not about performance or perfection. Its presence. And if you want a real connection, you have to participate.

It's practice. So go practice and stay curious.

The world needs more love between people who meet without expectation, extraction, or agenda. Just a genuine connection that feeds the soul and reminds us how good it feels to simply belong.

Chapter 7
Stop Chasing Happiness;
In Fact, Stop Chasing Anything

I've always been drawn to music, dance, painting, writing, and creating in any form. Losing myself in art never felt like a choice, more like a calling, a safe place where everything was possible. Writing, especially, has been my anchor. Lyrics, journal entries, poetry, stories, whatever the form, it felt like purpose, like I was doing the right thing for my well-being. As a child, I could recognize happiness simply by being in the moment. Every second I spent creating felt epic, iconic. By being fully in the moment, your body and soul connect with time, the most expansive aspect of our existence. Time is the continuous, irreversible progression of our existence. Happiness to me is being aware of that and not taking your time for granted.

Hear me when I say this: momentum is everything when you translate your spirit into the material world. And even though I was burnt out, tired, overextended, and at times depressed, I decided to stop ignoring the thoughts that kept circling in my mind — the ones that returned, whether I was awake or asleep. So I wrote them down. I exaggerated them. Pulled them apart. I gave them a home. I'm letting you into this home with a warm welcome. Here, we speak from our experience only, never from a place of superiority or complete knowing.

The day I was confronted with what I always thought happiness was, we were in Vienna. My second album, Moody Blues, had just entered the German charts at number 20. Everyone was in a celebratory mood, glancing at me with excitement and enthusiasm. I knew this was a huge milestone, but I drifted off. My body was not at that table. For someone like me, with my background, the challenges I had faced growing up, being nominated was a big deal. Nothing about me ever felt "typically German." The closest thing to German culture I knew was my mother's parenting style. And even she was treated like an outsider in her own family. It was a bit of a surprise to me that my work was so well-received in Germany. If anything, I was continuously expressing my otherness, and it pleasantly surprised me how many music lovers felt drawn to my work even though I was not singing in German.

My first album was a fairly understated success. I was nominated for an Echo Award and played shows internationally. I sang jazz, soul, and blues. I never wanted my voice to be pretty. I wanted it to be unforgettable. It didn't matter if you liked my work, but I noticed that my name came up in conversations about music and art. I was frequently invited to perform in prestigious settings and venues next to artists I admired. Erykah Badu, Asa, Marcus Miller, Esperanza Spalding, the list was long. Singers with perfect technique and angelic high notes surrounded me in the industry. It drove me insane. Why did everyone want to sound and look pretty? I couldn't relate. I didn't want to impress anyone. I wanted to express something. I looked up to Nina Simone, Tracy Chapman, Sade, and Dinah Washington. Artists who sang from their guts. Their voices didn't ask for approval. They were just felt. I admired that.

Back to that moment in Vienna. My entire team surrounded me. Representatives from the label, my manager, and some other individuals I didn't know well were present. So, when my publicist walked up to me that day and told me I'd charted, I smiled. I was gracious. I downed a glass of champagne, shoved two breakfast muffins into my mouth, congratulated everyone, said something tacky about dreams coming true, then went to the bathroom, stuck my fingers down my throat, threw everything up, rinsed my mouth, and smoked a cigarette out the window. In short, I felt like shit. And that terrified me. Wasn't I supposed to be happy? I was successful and respected; my music was being heard. And yet, I felt empty. You know you need to work on your trauma when everything you dreamt of happens, and it still doesn't feel like it's happening to you. My PTSD from childhood made sure I swapped bodies with the persona I created with the one on TV, the one nominated for awards. My eating disorder didn't come from wanting to be thin, it came from not wanting to feel myself at all. I wanted to disappear. I refreshed my lipstick and returned to the table, celebrating and getting increasingly drunk.

Whatever you think happiness is to you, my advice is to stop chasing it and become more aware of how you spend each moment of your day. How much intention are you implementing into your tasks? At the time, I didn't know how to make myself feel whole and present again. The more self-awareness I acquired, the heavier I became. I was collecting knowledge the way some people collect antiques, beautifully arranged and completely useless. I was drowning in insight. I had gathered so many thoughts about life, myself, and the world. However, I hadn't cracked the code for being fully present and truly enjoying my success. Let's address this head-on. You and me, right here, right now. This book is all about simplifying your life. I think life is wildly complex, as it should be. My attitude has always been to embrace the complexities. If something doesn't serve us emotionally, physically, or financially, we move swiftly in the direction of change, fully aware that something or someone doesn't serve us. We are the creators of our lives and take full responsibility for the world we create.

I don't believe in chasing the next thing and only feeling happiness through significant achievements. I have swapped that with purpose and intention, and life has become less complicated, filled with happier moments. Life should never be a competition. Not even with yourself. You are not a racehorse. This competition thing is the thief of joy. We're all winning and losing simultaneously. We all mess up in our own way. Life is designed to be unpredictable and complex. It's the dance between highs and lows, good times and bad, and that's where the magic lies.

If someone says, "All I want you to be is happy," reject it. Happiness won't fix your problems. Honesty will. How are you really feeling? Today, this moment, and any day. The key to surviving the chaos is accepting your humanity in a world that prefers efficient, functional humans who can work, produce, and fuel the economy at all times. Here's the first hack: stay humble. It doesn't matter how accomplished, intelligent, wealthy, or attractive you are. I also don't care how miserable or depressed you might feel. You're not better than anyone around you, and your suffering is no more intense than someone else's. Trust me, whenever you think it's bad for you, it's worse for someone else. That's the reality. That's what kept me going.

I often merge myself into the collective feeling of consciousness, fully accepting that we are all going through something and trying to emerge from the other side with all our bones intact. We're all one in that sense. There is no separation in human consciousness. So when you wonder, why can't we all live happily ever after, spreading peace and love? Let me tell you: the world is messy, and it won't get fixed by making everything about yourself. Life isn't fair. We either get lucky or we don't. You can be rich and still get sick one day. You can be poor, but you can still change the world. Nothing is fixed. Nothing stays the same. We're not in control. Life is like walking through a maze with blindfolds on, feeling your way to what might be the exit. Your senses sharpen, but in the end, you can only find the way out if you get lucky.

Humility is underrated. It brings you back to the physical reality of just being here. All you have to do is exist. Combine that with three deep breaths, and suddenly, the chaos doesn't feel so overwhelming. You'll get lucky. You'll stumble upon the exit. Keep telling yourself that, and let your body follow.

I'm an artist who got lucky. By working hard and being around the right people at the right time, I was able to turn my life into my world. And today, I'm grateful for every opportunity, for good health, and for the ability to express myself. Those are the foundations of happiness. Gratitude. From there, you can create anything. I've always felt immense gratitude, no matter how sad I felt on the inside. I've never resonated more with the Greek philosopher Socrates: "I know that I know nothing." That mindset keeps me curious, and curiosity is everything. I stay open to change, ready for challenges that broaden my perspective. I love learning new things. Do you? It's always been about seeking knowledge from the world around you, from conversations with people who think for themselves, who lead with their minds and bodies in a healthy, non-toxic way. It's beautiful to watch people succeed. Their success fuels my own curiosity and inspiration. So let go of the jealousy and envy. Try being genuinely happy for someone else. It works. And it's not that hard.

Happiness isn't a destination. It's a daily practice. If you think happiness is the goal, you're chasing an unsustainable feeling. The negativity, the setbacks, and the messiness of life matter just as much. Negative emotions spark change. They help you define boundaries. You can't recognize good feelings unless you've sat with the bad ones. Like when I was smoking out of the bathroom window in Vienna, realizing I had to work on myself. That awful moment gave me clarity. It pointed me toward healing.

There are two kinds of people: those who deny their negative emotions and those who deprive themselves of their positive ones. Both are dangerous. We need the full spectrum to survive, grow, and evolve. But don't forget, hope is the key. Studies show unhappiness sets in when you lose hope, when you stop believing in yourself. It's okay to seek help. You don't have to carry everything on your own. If you've lived through trauma, you deserve support. Therapy changed my life. I'm forever grateful to every skilled therapist who held space for my truth.

Happiness is not something you chase. It's something you nurture. If you feel it, you've just gotten lucky. And if you don't, it doesn't mean you're broken. It means you're alive. We all have the power to rewire and reset. Start by managing yourself, not the world. Dive into your feelings. See what they teach you. Remember, it's not always them. Sometimes it's you. And that's not an insult. It's a beginning. We all have the ability to activate pleasure, not through distractions or escapes, but through clarity and discipline. Maintaining a productive and balanced state of mind is the real flex. Even rest can be powerful if your intentions are aligned.

Satisfaction comes from overcoming, not avoiding, and moving through discomfort to earn your peace. So ask yourself, honestly. Are you satisfied? What's in your way? Are you finally ready to stop chasing happiness and start living? The world doesn't need more people chasing money and mistaking it for happiness. It needs those who move with purpose, who understand that joy is not something bought or won, but something felt. Real happiness flows from love, not the kind tied to applause or achievement, but the quiet, unwavering kind that lives in the heart. Love grows when we stop reaching for gold and start listening for truth. It reveals itself not in status, but in spirit.

The world needs more joy and inner peace radiating from those who understand that life moves in waves and nothing stays the same.

Chapter 8
Go Take a Nap

I remember being constantly tired. It was likely due to being on the road, waking up at ungodly hours to catch flights, and struggling to sleep after a show. When people asked me how I was, I would often brush it off and change the topic. I know I should have asked how they were and what had been happening in their lives, but sometimes I was just too tired and sad to do so. I was too tired to climb out of my own skin, let alone reach into someone else's. I was too drained to say, "I'm not okay; please be there for me."

It took me years to say that. To unlearn pride. To admit I couldn't do it alone. This is what depression does. It clouds your mind and makes you very tired. And the moment you lie down, you are unable to rest fully. I beat my depression because I believed there was a way through it: hope and conviction. There was more to life than this. I felt responsible for telling this part of my story because maybe someone out there would hear it and think, "This too shall pass." It will pass, darling. There is a way out of this.

I wrote my song "Diamonds" to remind myself that life was a treasure, a raw gem. God, or the angels, or some therapist wouldn't cut it. You cut it yourself. You polished it. You turned the pain into light. Even on my darkest days, I believed firmly that everyone had to take full responsibility for their own happiness. Life would end. Suddenly, stupidly, quietly. And when it did, would I be proud of how I lived? Or would I only realize too late that I was just surviving? I wanted to look back one day and say: That was a bumpy ride, but fuck it, I loved it.

My depression lasted a long time. It didn't sneak up on me like some people said. It attacked like a wild animal. I knew when it started. I was working on my second album. The first had done well.

I had made it. I was finally the rock star I always wanted to be. I was everywhere, performing in France, Italy, Poland, Switzerland, the United States, and the UK. If I was not performing, I was writing songs for myself or others.

But I was disappearing. My boyfriend, whom I'll refer to as X, looked at me one day and said, "You need to see a doctor." He wasn't wrong. I was done hiding the bulimia. I kept it quiet. Threw up in silence. Nothing about it felt extreme. It was mechanical. My private, violent self-harming routine. This little game I played to offload all the pain I felt inside. Where did it come from, this urge to vanish? To be thinner, cleaner, smaller, untouchable? For me, food became a language. I confused it with love, with pleasure, with comfort. I stuffed it into the empty, aching space that grew bigger every time I stood on stage, performing my songs and presenting my work.

One thing that helped me through it was napping and getting enough sleep. When I was napping, my mind was quiet. It did not work. It did not shake. It was silent. Yes, life was hard. Yes, it hurt. Yes, trauma cuts deep. But there was a way through. The first step? Admit it. Say it out loud: "I feel like shit." Then tell one or two people you trust. Most people don't know how to hold space for someone else's sadness. They say the wrong things. Or nothing at all. That's okay. I wasn't broken for needing help. I just needed to be smart about who I let in. I got help. A coach. A therapist. A healer. I treated my emotions like part of my body. My feelings were part of my health. And in between all of that, I made sure I got enough sleep. I loved those time-outs. They were essential. Therapy wasn't about weakness. It was about perspective. It was someone helping me understand that life, despite it all, was still worth living. That my past was real, but it wasn't my destiny. They helped me connect the dots. They reminded me I wasn't crazy. I was human. Healing is not a solo performance. And silence would have eaten me alive if I hadn't learned how to break it. Resting your body means resting your mind. Sleep is essential to anyone battling PTSD. I want to help you find your perfect sleep pattern. It saved my life. It can help you too.

We're all fed up. So now what? Let me remind you of something: remember how badly you wanted what you have now? Me too. It's wild how easy it is to forget. So, the next time you're about to spiral into one of your predictable nervous breakdowns, remind yourself of that. Preferably before you lose it completely. And then, take my advice: go take a nap. Yes, you heard me. Lie down for twenty minutes, close your eyes, and do absolutely nothing. Set a timer if you're worried about oversleeping. Whether you actually fall asleep or just drift for a while doesn't matter. The point is to tell your brain to switch off.

Think of yourself as a laptop with too many tabs open. What happens when the whole system freezes? Exactly. You shut it down. You don't try to keep clicking around; you reboot. That's precisely what a nap does for your mind and body. Close the damn tabs.

We seriously underestimate the importance of sleep. Sleep is not a luxury. It's life support. Skipping out on it isn't just ruining your mood; it's robbing you of years of your life. The connection between poor sleep and disease isn't speculation. It's science. Your memory, immune system, and mental health all depend on sleep. Those extra two hours you miss, yeah, they might be the difference between "I'm thriving" and "Please, don't talk to me today." While you're out cold, your body is busy saving your life. Your organs regenerate. Cells repair. And your brain, the most mysterious part of you, is finally resting. No forced thoughts. No overthinking. Just subconscious engineering, far away from your ego. Your ego. That loud, restless part of you that always wants to do, to control, to fix. Sleep shuts it up. And thank God for that. Without it, your body and mind don't get the full reset they desperately need.

Let's talk numbers. Less than seven to eight hours of sleep a night? You're setting yourself up for long-term health issues. But let's get real: not everyone has the privilege to manage their sleep. Class plays a massive role in how much rest we get. If you're working three jobs just to stay afloat, sleep isn't exactly a priority. It's a luxury. Compare that to someone who earns enough to live comfortably, with manageable working hours and no financial stress keeping them awake at night. It's not the same. The ability to regulate your sleep is a privilege. If you're one of the lucky ones who can control your schedule, don't take it for granted. Not everyone gets to choose.

Some people skip sleep because their hustle demands it, while others have no choice because life is relentless. Either way, recognize the privilege of being able to prioritize rest and use it wisely.

And while we're here, let's be honest. If you're doom-scrolling TikTok at 2 a.m., congratulations, you've declared war on your brain. Don't blame your bad mood the next day. That was all you. Now, let's talk about sleep killers. They're everywhere: alcohol, your phone, bad room temperature, racing thoughts, a snoring partner, crying babies, dirty sheets, heavy meals, wifi boxes, noise pollution, and even the wrong kind of breathing. The list is endless, but the solution is simple. Approach bedtime with intention. Take sleep as seriously as you take your ambitions, because without it, you won't get far. Think of sleep as the ultimate act of self-respect. In a world that glorifies sleepless hustle, you'll recharge and wake up ready to conquer while everyone else stumbles through their exhaustion. To this day, I place great importance on rest and sleep. Sleep saved me from my thoughts when I was depressed, and now it just fuels me. It feels like my body is updating during my mostly eight-to-ten-hour rest. I take my updates very seriously. You should too. Because the world doesn't need more burnt-out overachievers chasing their worth in chaos.

The world needs more rested, healthy individuals who honor their bodies, protect their minds, and know when to lie the hell down.

Chapter 9
We Are Not That Special and That's Okay

I should've been way more self-aware about my credibility as a songwriter in my twenties, but I wasn't. I didn't think much about success, and I just focused on the work. The mission was to write songs that reflected my artistic expression. That was it. Just because people liked what I did didn't automatically mean I was particularly good at it. It was always about getting better than my definition of good. Flattery is nice. But also a bit tacky. I never leaned on it, nor did I base my talent on it.

For me, it was always about the process, the experience, and the work itself. Early on, I played a considerable role in vocal production, song arrangement, and actual songwriting, but I rarely received any credit for it. At one point, I did get credit because my then-manager insisted on putting my producer credits on the record. I remember the producer I had worked with being extremely upset about that. Almost disappointed in me, convinced he was the only one who vocally produced me.

But here is my sincere question: how can you produce a singer who writes her own words and melodies?

I simply didn't know that other people usually did this. I also didn't care about being authentic or unique; I just was. And I'm still shocked to this day how hard some people try to portray something artistic or unique, yet it often feels forced and contrived, like a decoration to someone's character. I didn't understand when the label said to me, 'We need an image.' I was confused about what that even meant or represented.

I was relatively pure when I got signed, convinced it was all about the art, not the money. Only during the process did I realize this was a highly commercial business driven by numbers. I learned quickly to adapt and see the music industry for what it was. It was a business like any other that grew over time. Only the toughest survive, only the most creative survive, because this business is about reinvention, delivery, and adaptation.

It's also about how much money you make them, and that's fine, just not that special. Everything is about money anyway, especially when someone took a risk and believed in you. They put a big bet on you, and you can't and shouldn't disappoint them. As much as I feel like I'm unique in my way of being and thinking, I do not think I'm special. There are many others out there with new ideas and diverse cultural backgrounds. People are killing it out there. I'd never put myself above anyone, but I'd also never put myself beneath anyone.

I've always found this obsession with being special exhausting and unnecessary. You're not here to be someone else's ideal, you're here to be yourself. How can you then keep circling your thoughts around yourself? That will make anyone dizzy after a while. Who cares how others will perceive what you do or who you are? My experience with people is that they spend a tremendous amount of time thinking about themselves, losing complete perspective of what's out there or even right in front of them. I guess it's the delicate balance of staying in touch and out of touch with yourself.

I'm not expecting anyone to do something great and purposeful with their life. In fact, I find this trend of everyone wanting to feel special or exceptional quite tedious and redundant. It seems like the new fear unlocked for most people is being "normal." But what does that even mean? To have a normal job, live an everyday life, have normal opinions, or dress normally? Let me debunk this for you real quick. It's only "normal" if you define it as normal. And it's totally okay to be normal. I aspire to be normal most days. I look up to normal people. There is a beauty in just falling under the radar and doing everyday things. Nothing about the way we live now is normal. My great-grandparents would be rolling in their graves if they saw humanity's advancements in technology and science. What feels normal to you might be entirely absurd for someone else. I see so many people exuding entitlement because they're living a particular lifestyle or following what they think is a "special" path. Let me say this loud and clear: none of us is so special that we need to feel superior or inferior to anyone else. We are all living in our separate bubbles simultaneously, each of us concerned with things we deem important.

You're not better than your neighbor because you're an entrepreneur traveling the world in first class, and you're not worse off because you work a 9-to-5 and take the bus every day. I love taking the bus. I take it every chance I get. Looking out of a bus as it drives around town is exquisite. I love it. Thinking you're better than someone because of what you do, how much you earn, or where you've been is nothing but insecurity disguised as arrogance. True confidence doesn't need an audience. No one needs to see you while you are living life. As a performer, I know how meaningless applause can be if you are not happy with yourself. Never do anything for applause. Do it for the love.

Try not to put yourself in a mental position where you believe your situation is so unique that it requires special attention.

I've never understood the concept of looking down or up at people. Nothing is ever as it seems. Some of the wealthiest people are the most depressed, and some of the poorest are the most creative and content. You are not here to compare yourself to anyone or live up to their projections. You need to stop feeling like you deserve more or less than others. At the core, we're all just people trying to make it through life. The labels we slap on ourselves, entrepreneur, artist, 9-to-5 worker, don't mean a damn thing if we lose sight of our humanity. What type of person are you when it comes to doing the right thing? Are you kind? Are you fair? Life surely isn't, but are you? What have you done for your community? Way more interesting in my opinion. These are things that could potentially make you special, your ability to spread joy and kindness into a world that desperately needs it.

The best approach is to acknowledge that there is always room for improvement. Growth isn't about doing something grand or flashy; it's about looking in the mirror and asking, "What am I choosing today that brings me closer to my best self?" And if the answer is "nothing," then it's time to choose again.

You're good where you are. Your only job is to improve and grow at your own pace. Take the pressure off. Nobody needs to feel sorry for you or treat you differently. Think about it. In interviews with disabled individuals, they often say all they want is to be treated "normally." I've never forgotten that. These are people who have had it harder than most, and yet their only request is dignity and respect, because that should be the norm. Meanwhile, it feels like everyone else wants so much without putting in the work. The internet gives us the illusion that we've "made it" just because one of our clips went viral. Fuck that. The most interesting and beautiful people you'll ever meet are the ones who don't care about being interesting or beautiful. They're too busy creating change within themselves and serving others.

Stop trying to feel special. Stop trying to be special. Start focusing on growth. And if you're someone who wants to stand still and stay where you are in life, that's fine too. But don't judge others who aspire to create something different for themselves.

Being normal doesn't mean being mediocre; it means being grounded. It means living your truth without the constant need to prove it. And trust me, that's rare enough to be extraordinary.

The world needs more normal people. People who value kindness and compassion. Those who don't strive to stand out, but who stand within and stand up for their community, improving the lives of others and making the earth a more livable place for humankind to survive and thrive.

Chapter 10
Turn Your Rage into Action

What do you do when you miss your father, but the truth is, missing him is the only good thing he's ever given you? So you stay there. Suspended in the ache. An empty desire to feel whole. Because life gets heavy, and deep down, you want to know what you're made of. What tools do you have to survive the weight?

But that's adulthood. No one hands you a manual. You grow up. You grow into yourself. Into the discomfort. The anger. The silence. And some days, you let the sadness take over. You retrieve and cry. You let your shadows move through you, dark and heavy, and lean into the ritual of release. Loneliness, rage, grief. All of it. Because the moment you tell yourself the truth, everything begins to shift. The world opens up in a way it never did before. And for the first time in a long time, you feel a flicker of freedom.

It was over. I had lived my childhood. More importantly, I had survived it. And with that, I carried all the lived experience and every lesson it taught me. The good. The brutal. The in-between. I made a decision to move forward without bitterness. But to do that, I had to unlearn a lot.

I remember sitting at a bar with X. Still sober, more interested in the peanuts than the wine. "I don't want to wake up every morning thinking about my past," I said. "It's strange. I'm young, healthy, full of energy, and yet I keep going back to how complex and painful my childhood was." X nodded. "We've all seen shit," he said. "Sometimes it just… comes up. That's normal." I know it well. The way old memories crash through your brain, uninvited. You freeze. Swallow hard. And wonder, do I go deeper or run? Sometimes, you have to go deeper. Music helped me. It gave the pain somewhere to go. It gave me a voice when I didn't want to speak. That's why I share it. Not because I think I'm special, but because I know I'm not the only one who feels, remembers, or survives.

When I look at photos of myself as a child, it feels like I'm looking at a distant cousin. Familiar, but not quite me. There's a strange gap between who I was and who I've become. To understand my subconscious, I had to confront the person I used to be. That meant revisiting pain. Sitting with it. Letting it speak. Gaining distance. It was uncomfortable. Slow. Necessary.

And no, you can't do it alone. You'll try. You'll fail. You'll get angry. Very angry. Don't let anyone tell you the past doesn't matter. It does. It lingers. It creeps in like smoke under the door.

When I was fifteen, I stayed up all night writing. I drank coffee, skipped school, and didn't sleep. I didn't know how to process my anger, so I made art.

Music, dance, writing. Anything that could carry the weight for me. I was heartbroken that my parents didn't work out, and angry at both of them for dragging me through the wreckage.

That kind of pain followed me for years. If you're not careful, pain turns into numbness, numbness into despair, despair into hopelessness, hopelessness into self-hate, and self-hate into quiet self-destruction. I didn't know how to treat myself with love because love didn't match how I felt on the inside.

When we were kids, we were unfiltered. We let out our emotions in ways that were sometimes uncanny and, most of all, very direct. Have you ever seen a child throw a fit in the mall? You can feel their pain and rage without even knowing them. It's powerful. I'm in awe of that. I remember getting so furious as a child. I was an annoying little girl with extreme moods and all sorts of perceptions of how I needed things to be. From my toys, which I had carefully arranged on my bed, to my murals, the solar system I had painted on my walls, to the little songs I composed on my Casio. If things didn't go my way, I simply lost my cool. There is something so punk and poetic about that.

Remember being that young? When we felt sadness, we cried or withdrew. When we felt happiness, we laughed or danced around. When we felt anger, we cried, shouted, or kicked everything in sight.

Then the years passed, parenting kicked in, and society merged us into its mold. We learned it wasn't sweet or acceptable to express our anger publicly. Unless in a romantic situation. There is something quite poetic about yelling at each other on a street corner, drunk, vulnerable, oversensitive, and most likely horny. I dated this one guy once. We used to fight all the time. It was like a choreographed foreplay to great passionate sex, which never resolved the problem, which was that we were just not good for each other.

Think about your teenage years. Your body was changing, your hormones were all over the place, and you were just trying to make sense of it all. You experienced intense emotions, such as joy, sadness, and anger, with nowhere to escape them. I personally believe people create their best work between the ages of 17 and 30. After that, it's luck or sheer willingness to hold on to that childlike and teenage energy. Where there are pure and raw emotions, there is an intensity that is felt with writers, artists, and singers that is undeniably infectious. I firmly believe that I created my best work in my teens and twenties. I never want to go back there, though. Trying to replicate a certain emotion or feeling at a more advanced age is tacky. Like a self-fabricated midlife crisis. As in, it is totally "mid" to try and be who you were. It's like middle-aged men coming in in a full streetwear outfit because that's who they used to be. I firmly believe in acting your age. Whatever that means for different people.

How many times has your rage helped you take constructive action, and how many times has it blocked you from what you wanted simply because you were not in control of it? Rage is a transmuting energy, a force that tells you when you've had enough, when your emotions try to guide you through the next tunnel of sentiments. It's the signal that something has to change.

How many times have you gotten angry and finally had the courage to leave a toxic situation or set a much-needed boundary? Society labels anger as an ugly emotion, but here's my theory: depression is just suppressed rage. When a depressed person stops being angry, that's when it gets dangerous. Not only for the person who feels that anger, but also for the people around them. The battle with yourself or the world clears the ground for something new, but can be destructive when not attended to in a creative, solution-oriented way. I remember being part of a panel at a music industry conference and saying: Art is war. You kind of have to be at war with yourself or with the world to create something of relevance. I've experienced that being an artist is made of being in pain or trying to avoid that pain by expressing yourself.

Anything you can't change will make you sad. When you can't translate your emotions into words, art, or action, sadness takes over. But change equals life. We're meant to evolve. Just like nature, we have seasons; we bloom and wilt, depending on the conditions around us. Mutability is essential for our survival. Nature is the most honest teacher. Never forget that.

Maybe your anger shows up in small ways: that coworker who interrupts you in meetings, the friend who always takes but never gives, or the driver going slow in the fast lane when you're already late. These little moments build up, and if you don't release that anger, it stays inside, spreading like poison.

Your anger and sadness, when used correctly, are a catalyst. It sparks confrontations, ends bad situations, and opens new possibilities. Start viewing it as that before you get into a toxic cycle of suppression and denial. I always found nothing more pleasing than the calm I felt after drawing a big cross on a piece of paper and setting it on fire. The cross stood for my anger, and the fire stood for my power of knowing how to transmute negative emotions.

I've always asked myself why anger is so unpopular. As I mentioned earlier, I loved it as a child. I imagined a storm brewing every time I got angry. I realized how relaxing it felt after I let out my anger through a scream or fists into my pillow. Even as a little girl, I was able to say NO with my entire chest, without feeling bad. Storms calm down, leaving the sky clearer than ever. The same is true for us. Anger is the storm, but clarity follows, giving us ease, inspiration, and something new to start from.

So, when was the last time you checked in with your anger? When was the last time you admitted that anger is part of our human experience and not acknowledging it will only make it fester, or even worse, be expressed by letting it out on others? When did you last give yourself the space to feel it fully? Suppressed emotions manifest physically in your muscles, your skin, and your health. The key is to release that anger before it turns into destruction. There is nothing more unproductive and dangerous than unprocessed anger. There is something quite arousing about anger. It's taboo, it's not proper, it is complicated. Experiment with it and see what you can find.

How often have you clenched your jaw and said, "It's fine," when it wasn't? How frequently have you smiled through frustration because it wasn't "the right time" to speak up? We've all been there and paid the price for pretending it's "fine." When people say, "I'm fine," with their clenched teeth and squinting eyes, I often want to reply: Yes, we are all fine. Now, let's all jump out of the window or something.

I'm not suggesting you dismantle your apartment or scream at everyone who annoys you. I'm suggesting awareness. Feel that first surge of anger and ask yourself: Why? What can I do for myself right now to soothe these emotions without hurting myself or anyone around me? Be bold about it. Be honest for once. It would be so lovely for your brain. I wish I had been courageous about my anger. Too often, I let it out on myself, my soul, and my mind.

Here's what I do now: scream into a pillow, cry in the bathroom, or write into a diary to decipher the cause. Complete unfiltered honesty on paper is the best way to release negative emotions. Sometimes I talk to someone I trust to structure my thoughts. I paint, I sing, I dance. Sometimes I do nothing, I just want to feel it.

The worst thing you can do is let anger simmer into passive-aggressiveness. That energy blocks transformation and repels good things. It's also quite annoying to be around a passive-aggressive person who simply is incapable of channeling their emotions into direct communication. If you have a problem, say it. Talk about it. Express yourself. I'm always surprised how many grown adults cannot express themselves directly, respectfully, and calmly.

I've cultivated the habit of confronting people openly and directly. I look them in the eye, express myself without smiling, laughing, attacking, or raising my voice, and tell them how I feel. No attack, just observation. I give them the chance to explain what they are going through or clarify their problem. Sometimes people have a problem with you, and that's okay, too. It's your right to discover why someone is acting strangely towards you. Unless you don't care, of course. Always let it go if you find out that you don't give a fuck. That goes without saying.

I've also learned to let anger pass through me. If I'm too overwhelmed, I reschedule appointments, stay in the house, and binge-watch Mary Poppins, Kill Bill, and Sex and the City. Odd combination, I know. But it makes me feel good. If someone I love isn't hearing me, I make sure they feel it. Sometimes, people need that. I believe it is necessary to respond with the same energy with which you are confronted, as I learned from my dear friend. Some people are just not willing to learn or self-correct. If that's the case, give them what they deserve: a reflection of themselves. It comes in handy that most people are self-absorbed and only learn if you mirror their same behavior, for them to recognize their own patterns.

Control is essential. Catch your emotions before they catch you. People who repeatedly offload their anger onto others or act like everything is fine are weak in different ways. Neither approach shows self-respect or boundaries. Growing up with a father who could erupt with unreasonable anger at times made me realize how little control he had over himself and his energy.

Anger isn't the enemy; it's a compass. It's your secret weapon. Your frustration with your job might push you to update your resume. Your annoyance with a toxic friendship might inspire you to set boundaries. That argument with your partner might be your wake-up call to communicate better.

Use anger as a tool. Scream into the forest and see which bird responds to you, write that email (and delete it), or take a walk while angrily muttering to yourself. Just don't let it simmer. Never internalize your anger. You are a beautiful being, entitled to inner peace and freedom. Do not let anger take over your existence.

I already told you to be angry. Now I'm telling you to transform your anger into something productive. Do not ignore it. Do not let it rule you. Use it. Master it. Apply it. Transform it. Oh, and just put it to work.

The world needs more people who don't run from what hurts. Who let it burn, learn from the fire, and still choose not to set the world on fire with them.

Chapter 11
Boundaries and Choices

Late nights, no sleep. Working overtime just to avoid going home. There was nothing there. Being alone felt like work. I couldn't bear to go home and sit in silence. I stayed in X's bed. He set up a mic on the nightstand, so close I could still feel the warmth of the sheets as I whispered into it, recording songs before the dream entirely faded.

When I listen back to my third album, Mermaid Blues, all I hear is a woman trying to break out of her shell while still running back to it every time things get complicated. Songs like Sunday and Take Him Back were written in bed. I was hiding and breaking open at the same time. The room smelled like lavender oil and stale coffee, the air always a bit too warm. I didn't care. Everything felt like an experiment, a lucid dream about how far I could push myself. Write three songs a day? Sure. Get on a plane every three days to play shows? Why not. Anything to avoid the stillness that waited for me in the dark.

I was always tired. Always drained, blending into my surroundings like smoke. So when someone said something disrespectful or outrageous, I just nodded and said, Sure. I didn't have the energy to argue or defend myself. There were no boundaries left in my body to protect. I was too detached from myself, too exhausted by the pressure I kept piling on. I've always been terrible at setting boundaries, which is probably why I consider myself an expert now. I grew up with two headstrong parents, each with firm ideas about how I should navigate life. Moving between different worlds, speaking several languages, absorbing countless cultural codes, I lost track of where I ended and the world began. Adaptation demands openness. You observe, absorb, and translate. But it also makes it easy to lose sight of who you are. If you're not careful, you become a mirror for everything but yourself.

I've already mentioned that both my parents were emotionally complex. It would erupt here and there when there was too much stress and alcohol involved. Very out of fashion. Vulnerability, softness, empathy. Those things barely existed. Even as a teenager, it was about pushing through, no matter what came my way. Typical, I guess. Back then, I was always cool with everything because I didn't know how to confront or enforce my limits. Did I even know what a limit was? And, to be honest, I also wanted to be liked. I wanted to be that person who never made a fuss, never caused a scene. Looking back, it's laughable. But it makes sense. When you grow up in a house where conflict explodes without warning, you end up terrified of it. You start to believe that speaking up will trigger chaos. So you stay quiet. You act cool. You let things slide. I find it deeply unsettling now when I meet someone who's constantly fine, never disrupting anything for fear of confrontation. The fear of conflict can erode our character and personality. There is no friction to our existence. It feels good, but it ultimately deprives us of progressing in our personal space. We become agreeable and forgiving, mostly to our own detriment.

Some people are triggered by the parts of us we've outgrown but still carry old wounds, unresolved patterns, and familiar pain. Let me offer clarity: you attract what you internalize. If you mistreat yourself or allow others to mistreat you, you invite more of the same. Boundaries are not walls; they're filters. They keep your energy clean and your path aligned.

I like to split boundaries into two categories. First, the ones you set with yourself. Second, the ones you set with others. Both rest under the umbrella of accountability. Know yourself well enough to stop betraying your own values. Only then can you stop others from doing the same. Read this again. The truth is a funny concept if you let it amuse your brain. The conscious decision to be intentional about your boundaries will be a milestone in your personal development that you don't want to miss. And no, being 'nice' to the point where you turn into a human doormat is not a virtue; it's self-sabotage. It changed my life to fully understand that I have free will and that I can make the choice to step up for myself every single day.

When was the last time you checked in with your self-care? Not the curated version. The real one. Did you sleep, or are you coasting on caffeine, cocaine, and denial? Eating anything green, or just grabbing whatever's fast and numbing? How's your hair, your nails, your skin? Are they holding you together or barely hanging on? Are you counting drinks, or just assuming your liver will handle it? Do you even think about your liver? Are you actually moving through your to-do list, or just perfecting the art of procrastination? Is your solitude healing, or are you calling isolation "me time" to avoid admitting you feel alone? "Rotting" isn't a lifestyle, it's a symptom. It's what people call it when they've stopped trying but still want to be seen. Be honest. How much of your day is lost to scrolling? When was the last time you felt your brain stretch for something like curiosity, courage, or clarity? Or are you still Googling "how to fix my life" like that's going to save you? And what about kindness? Real kindness. When did you last do something for someone else without a craving for credit?

I ask because this is the mirror. How we treat ourselves is exactly how others learn to treat us. Nothing more, nothing less. There's no multiverse of you. There is only one you, which means you have to take full responsibility for what you do, or don't do. Taking care of yourself emotionally and physically is the bare minimum for setting boundaries with yourself and others. You don't owe anyone the truth about your life, but you definitely owe it to yourself to admit what's really going on. I was someone who took it to extremes before my body and mind broke down. You don't have to do the same.

Expressing yourself clearly is the next step. When was the last time you actually told someone what you needed instead of hoping they'd read your mind? Swallowed your frustration instead of standing up for yourself, only to explode over something small? Avoided saying no because you didn't know how, even though you're a full-grown adult with a working vocabulary? Boundaries are not just about saying no; they're about knowing who you are and expecting others to respond to that. Life is messy. Misunderstandings are part of it. Stop cutting people off and start speaking up. My decision to always speak up and advocate for myself and my well-being has not only improved my mental and physical health but has also led me to my tribe. Like-minded people who feel inspired by my presence, while still loving me enough to hold me accountable when I'm wrong.

How often do you let things slide to avoid conflict, only to erupt later over something trivial? Saying no isn't rude, it's responsible. You're not a toddler learning how to speak. You know what you want, so say it. Seek clarity.

If you don't know where you end and others begin, how can anyone else? Misunderstandings are part of life, but silence creates distance.

The world needs more people who wake up in the morning and utilize their free will, who choose themselves while peacefully expressing their needs and expectations to others. Confrontation does not need to turn into hostility. It can be a beautiful way to explore your boundaries and help others understand you better.

Chapter 12
Trust Yourself Before Anybody Else

It felt so easy to trust him. We were standing in the rain. His body pressed to mine, my brain melting from all the romance and cinematography. My life was unfolding into a movie. Those eyes locked on mine, his words exactly what I had always wished my father would say. He was a god I couldn't stop staring at, a masterpiece of my imagination and restless desire. Nothing he said sounded wrong, nothing he did made me question him. Finally, I thought, I could love. Love the idea that someone would catch me if I fell. That I wasn't alone. That I didn't have to fend for myself anymore. Finally, I could move further away from myself to avoid feeling the pain of just being sad about the fact that I love my father so deeply, without ever being able to establish a loving relationship, so I attached myself to the next man who offered me some familiarity; the pattern of loving men who were unavailable to me.

Once your self-esteem has been fractured by betrayal, by trauma, by the drastic erosion of your own reflection, you start trusting whatever offers relief.

The predator can feel like a companion if you are not accustomed to receiving love from your father. The man who constantly rages and fights the world. The man you love, regardless, because you are a part of him. The man who loved us when he was drunk and fought us when he got scared. Because you are his daughter. Because your body is programmed to love those who give you life. As an adult, I kept making wrong decisions, not because I wanted to, but because it soothes the ache of not feeling anything at all. When you constantly feel war in your home, you become numb. You choose to neutralize your needs and wants. When your intuition's been tampered with, illusions start to feel like home. You're not choosing alignment, peace, and love because you don't know it. I was never single. I was choosing escape over health. Because no one ever taught you how to rest inside yourself without shame and fear.

The moment I saw it for what it was, I said it out loud:

Bullshit. I need to stop.

If I had trusted myself even an inch more, I would've saved time. Real time. I would've hired better lawyers and made bolder career moves. And with men, I would've recognized sooner that most of them weren't saviors or kings, just projections of an old, unmet need. Pretenders and predators readily take advantage of my inability to create space for my needs, promising rescue but cutting into the same old wound kick-started by a father who only showed up when it served him.

I handed over my peace to men who never earned it, hoping they could fix what was never theirs to fix. Trusting them was easy. Trusting myself? That's where I seemed to fail.

Let's not pretend: many people are driven by motives that have nothing to do with your well-being. It's uncomfortable, but true. Concern is often performative, and loyalty is conditional. Communication and unity are easily sacrificed on the altar of ego, envy, and subtle sabotage. Even when it just happens on a subconscious level, it still happens.

Humans are wired for self-preservation. We often look out for ourselves first, even if it means lying, withdrawing, or letting someone down. That's why self-reliance isn't a suggestion; it's human nature. No matter how intoxicating the love, no matter how connected you feel, trust yourself first. Your intuition is the alarm that goes off before the damage is done. Mine now shows up in my solar plexus area. Placed between the navel and the chest, around the pit of the stomach, there's something I've always felt intensely. You know when you touch your navel and it tickles in your whole body? Anatomically, it's a network of nerves, yes, but to me, it's the center of my universe. It's a place where I experience things I can't explain. A kind of knowing that doesn't come from the five senses. I don't hear it, see it, or touch it, but I feel it. Deeply. It responds to moments that have nothing to do with logic. The flip when something feels off. The tension when someone is lying to me. The lightness when I'm aligned. Science might call it a bundle of nerve fibers, but I know it as something else entirely. A gateway. A signal post. The place where my instincts live before my brain catches up. Therapy helped unlock these parts of me. And crying. Letting go of guilt and shame. It's okay to talk about how domestic violence affected me. It's not taboo. I constantly need to remind myself of that. Some people say the soul isn't real. That's fine. I've felt mine in my stomach for years now.

I've felt grief, fear, intuition, and joy all rise from the same place. You can call it spiritual or psychosomatic, I don't care. It's real to me. And that's enough.

I've ignored my instincts more than once. Usually, for someone beautiful, charismatic, and deeply unavailable. A handsome guy with perfect timing and impeccable seduction skills. I'd get the signal, this is dangerous, don't go there, and still dive in. Most times, I got hurt. At other times, I was the one doing the hurting. Because when you abandon your own instincts, compassion becomes a luxury you can't afford.

Give yourself the space to be real, so you're not projecting your desires or trauma onto others. Pay attention. Really look at the people around you, partners, friends, family. What do their eyes say? Are they fidgeting? Do they interrupt to steer the conversation back to themselves? Most people don't want to connect; they want to distract themselves. They want to convince everyone, including themselves, that they're fine and just living life.

Let's get one thing straight. I didn't write this book to talk about myself, but sometimes context is necessary. I've always been curious about people, what they hide, what they show, and the contradictions in between. Everyone and everything has a place in my world. Judgment doesn't interest me much, unless you harm children or exploit vulnerable women. That's where tolerance ends and judgment begins.

When I was younger, I worked as a background vocalist. One of the band members nicknamed me "flavor" because I brought calm, peaceful energy into chaotic spaces. I listened, made people laugh, and avoided conflict. However, the truth was that I hated it. I hated working for others, putting myself second, and pretending everyone mattered when they didn't. I was just too complacent to admit that to myself.

Here's what I learned: if you act like an open canvas, people will draw all over you. They'll confuse kindness with naivety and treat you like a pushover. It took me longer than it should've to figure that out. Why? Because we live in a world where survival comes first. Unstable economies, rapid digitization, and constant adversity all contribute to a culture of selfishness. Trust, kindness, and love are luxuries most can't afford to give anymore.

Trust is such a rare currency. Entire empires are built on it. Family businesses thrive because trust is often passed down through generations. Creative teams flourish when it's the foundation. Without it, everything collapses, slowly or all at once. When I met my now husband, the first thing I said to him wasn't romantic. I said, "Work with me." I needed new management, and more than that, I needed someone I could trust. That's where the infamous line came from: I don't need a boyfriend, I need a manager. I meant every word. I wanted to test the depth of our connection through work. Shared pressure has a way of revealing who someone really is. In collaboration, you don't just see a person's talent; you see their timing, ethics, patience, ego, and flaws. It's the quickest way to meet someone in their most valid form.

Trust is not a given; it's a currency, earned, not assumed. When someone says, "Just trust me," take a step back. That's not reassurance, it's master manipulation. Your trust is not cheap; it's your intuition speaking, and that deserves reverence. Observe people. Test their consistency. Let them earn their place, both personally and professionally.

Stop oversharing with people who haven't earned the right to know your story. Ask more questions instead of offering up your life on a plate. Keep new friendships light and surface-level. Send the man you just met home at 10 p.m. Don't book vacations with someone after two dates.

Trust starts with you. Strengthen your inner compass. Meditate. Spend time alone. Make lists. Talk to people who've earned your trust instead of those who are just convenient. Learn to activate your inner voice.

The world needs more individuals who cannot be bought, broken, or brainwashed. Who trust their gut more than the echo of other people's projections.

Chapter 13
Shut Up and Listen

A lot of what I do is about listening. Listening to my body, the melodies in my mind, the songs that live inside my feelings, the odd little moments I share with strangers waiting for a train, listening to their convos and travel noises, the numbing soundtrack of big cities. It's a lot. But my body and mind are tuned to it, trying to turn it all into words, sounds, melodies. Music is everywhere: the way someone you love says your name, birds arguing in the morning, trees swaying like backup dancers, metal scraping, heels clicking down the street. Life is the best track I've ever heard. And honestly, we'd all be better off if we listened to each other and the world around us, the way we listen to a song we can't stop playing.

If you've made it this far, you're not here by accident. Whether it was curiosity or fate, something in you is searching. Searching for depth in a world obsessed with surfaces. That's unique and luxurious, like a moment of silence that doesn't feel empty. I didn't always have that silence. It came to me during lockdown, when time slowed and distractions fell away, no parties, no gatherings, no shows. I was finally left alone with my thoughts, and they didn't come gently. They asked hard questions. Most of what surrounds us is designed to steer us away from ourselves, to dilute instinct, to sedate emotion, to make obedience feel like peace. But the self, the true self, demands confrontation. And that is where clarity begins. The more you comply, the easier it is to manage you. Entire industries are built on your disconnection. On your impulse to please. On your hesitation to ask questions. You're expected to work harder, feel less, buy more, and say thank you while doing it. As much as I believe in being grateful, I want you to be thankful for the things that contribute to your health. Maybe you're in the middle of a beautifully packaged collapse, and somewhere along the way, you convinced yourself to smile through it. Well done. But are you okay?

For me, the turning point came without applause. I had been in the music industry for years, moving through every layer of it, but something shifted. The energy became mechanical, rehearsed, and predictable. The bigger the shows, the more opinions. More money, more pressure. I found it all very predictable and scary. I am in it for the art, the art of sound and emotions. My instincts were still sharp, but my identity no longer felt like my own. Many people were involved in my image and work. Talented people, opinionated people. They spoke over me, to me, and against me. They just did their job. I'm deeply in love with everyone who helped me elevate my career, but I needed a new language, a new narrator.

I needed myself. That realization arrived like a lucid dream. Slowly, I carried my dreams into the day. I dreamt in hotel rooms, on tour buses, and in soundproof recording rooms, where I felt present but no longer alive. I dreamt of being free. Some people called it madness, told me I was walking away from success, from everything I had worked for. I listened, nodded, and left anyway. Not out of defiance, but because I knew if I didn't reclaim my voice, I would lose the part of me that still believed in the miracle of creating something real and genuine for my fans, whom I loved so much, without being consumed by the thought of whether it was going to "sell". This music is who I am, and I am not for sale.

That's how Part 4: The Witch was born. It was an act of reclamation. I wasn't chasing or wanting anything with this album. I was choosing myself. The album is a mirror, reflecting grief, clarity, rebellion, softness, and the strength of remembering who you are, rather than being bedazzled by fame and money. No one can manipulate me into believing that money and popularity are the only ways to validate someone's talent. The witch, to me, is the purest symbol of female autonomy. She doesn't ask, she doesn't wait, she simply knows. In a music industry obsessed with packaging and approval, she is the force that creates outside the system. Untamed, unfunded, unbothered. She disrupts, transforms, and alchemizes. That's the pulse of the record. I didn't want to be marketed as a version of myself. I wanted to own the original. And independence didn't just give me creative control, it gave me spiritual precision. I listened to myself. It didn't make me popular within the industry, but I still left my mark. People knew that I knew what it felt like to be young, gifted, and free. There is nothing more powerful than spiritual clarity.

Seeing how people constantly contribute to their own unhappiness, making choices that don't bring them happiness, only made me more determined to get into their minds through my music and words. I never wanted people to idolize me or follow me, but I would like to offer practical, applicable wisdom. Things I needed to hear in my darkest hours. And maybe I'm a little superficial, because who doesn't love some good old tequila wisdom by an artist who just lives life?

Let's talk about Capitalism. Yeah, I said it. A system where money runs the show, and the more you make, the more control you get. It rewards those who play the game well, but the game itself is profit over people, power over ethics. Businesses compete, prices rise, and you're trained to keep buying. Those at the top keep getting richer while the rest keep running just to stay afloat. Work, earn, spend, repeat. The system thrives on you never feeling like you are enough, always reaching for more. In theory, sure, you're free to carve your own path, survival of the fittest, yey. Capitalism sells you the dream of success and forgets to mention the cost. Some make it, some burn out trying. Inequality grows, but hey, it's all in the name of growth and opportunity. Blah blah. This system thrives on disconnection, disconnection from your body, your gut feelings, your own damn voice. It needs you to be insecure, distracted, on meds, and hungry for things that don't actually nourish you. Curated ads being blasted onto your black mirror scream that you need fixing. Prices rise while joy, or just spending time with your family and friends, becomes a luxury. People are lonelier than ever. People are unhappier than ever, and it shows, as we now all have a platform to showcase our "happy" little lives. We are all scrolling, reposting, and mimicking authenticity. Fun. We are sending memes instead of speaking to each other, consuming instead of feeling, comparing instead of observing.

But you're here. Congratulations. How are you today? You've made it to this chapter because something inside you knows there's another way.

Feeling and listening to yourself in connection with human experience. That freedom of being able to sit alone and hear your thoughts and gut feelings express themselves to you in a language only you can comprehend. You are never alone. You are never lost.

The real gift is being able to listen to yourself before the noise of the world drowns out your purposeful attempt to live your life. A healthy life that serves you peace and comfort, even if it's boring, unspectacular, and not lived to impress or showcase.

Loving yourself means prioritizing your health. Whatever you're trying to achieve, do it from a place of fulfillment, not frustration, that endless, grinding frustration that comes from playing a role you were never meant to play. Life's complicated- as it should be. You wouldn't appreciate the good if everything were always easy. Sometimes, you have to march through the dark to come out the other side. Cliché? Maybe. True? Absolutely.

Let's get you to the point where you actually dare to listen to your body before you follow what your mind screams at you from a fear-driven, stressed, and sleep-deprived place. Your body is your master. And no, that's not some yoga meme wisdom; that's real-life shit. We need to create an atmosphere where your body comes first.

But what does that even mean? It means decoding what your body is trying to tell you. Trauma lives in all of us. Some people get lucky, they recognize it, work through it, and stop letting survival mode run their lives. Others? Not so lucky. They live numb, reactive, and functional, mostly being sad and bitter about something that happened to them in the past or about to happen to them in the future. They become defensive and closed off, not able to transcend their heavy feelings into actual life force.

I've been there. Living in a reactionary state of mind is like constantly putting out fires while accidentally lighting new ones. You're too busy surviving to actually be present. Pain is contagious, just like joy. It's addictive, just like joy.

Now I can already hear you asking, where do I start? Nowhere. You can't just flip a switch and heal your inner child, teen, or adult. And therapy? No guarantees there either. But here's the thing, you've already started. Way before you even decided to start. Your whole life is proof that you've been trying to navigate these messy, complex emotions, self-doubt, frustration, disappointment, impatience, entitlement, anxiety, and anger. All of it.

The gentle reminder is: all those feelings? You have to welcome them. Fully. That's the only way to recognize them. I want you to accept that you are complex and mysteriously radical. We all are. We're driven by emotions in a world that keeps telling us to suppress them if we want to "succeed". But suppressing isn't succeeding. It's surviving. And we're aiming for more than that.

According to the World Health Organization, about 70% of people globally experience at least one traumatic event in their lifetime. Trauma shows up differently for everyone. Not everyone ends up with PTSD, but that doesn't mean you're fine just because you're functioning. So, where do you actually start? Acknowledgment. Acknowledge that something, big or small, has shaped you. After that? It's up to you. Your body will tell you when something's off. Your skin, your gut, your energy. Pay attention. Chronic pain, stress, anxiety, irritability, that nagging sense that you're not really living, these are your body's alarm bells.

More money won't fix it. A shiny new thing won't fix it. A new relationship? Won't fix it. Alcohol and drugs? They will make it worse.

Being fully aware and accepting that work needs to be done will move you toward a more loving and productive relationship with yourself. So, when will you admit that?

I think now's a good time.

Therapy tailored to you, whether professional therapy, journaling, meditation, or just finally getting enough sleep, can help you reprogram your subconscious and reveal things you didn't even know about yourself. But it takes time, acceptance, and readiness.

Knowing yourself is the most badass thing you can achieve.

So start listening to your body. Stop letting your mind shout over it. Pay attention to what hurts and what triggers you. Your emotions want to be felt. Your body wants to be nurtured. It deserves to be put first. Because it's the vessel that carries you through life, and if that vessel sinks, no amount of success will keep you afloat. You don't want to be wealthy and successful in your dream house with a bad mood and attitude. It's not cute. It won't make you happy.

Listening to your body first isn't optional; it's mandatory. The world needs more people who listen to what they keep trying to avoid hearing: their inner voice.

Chapter 14
Love and Evolve

Like many women, I used to think the man who wanted me the most must love me the most. I was wrong. Sometimes a man wants you simply because you're available, not because he's capable of loving you. I've seen men mistake obsession for connection and settle for whoever happens to be standing closest when their ego gets hungry. There's often a wild disconnect between a man's mind, heart, and genitals. Like three departments that forgot they're supposed to be on the same team. I'm not saying every man, but this goes for many men I've come across. Nothing should ever be measured by how much men want something. It really doesn't mean anything. Some of their urges and instincts are way more rudimentary than we make them out to be.

Women tend to be more attuned to their emotions and more nuanced in their understanding of why they want something or someone. That's because most of us have been conditioned, from an early age, to overthink our desires, question our intentions, and justify our emotions. We weren't allowed to move blindly through the world. We had to explain ourselves, defend ourselves, and earn our space in nearly every room. This over-awareness is rooted in the patriarchal structures we've adapted to; systems that historically punished women for having agency, for doing their own thing, for simply existing outside the script. That kind of social training turns you into an analyst of people, of situations, of your own heart. We don't just feel, we interrogate the feeling.

Every time I was laid next to a man after mind-blowing sex, I convinced myself that this was love. It felt good, so it had to be love, right? Please! Only because he made you come a few times, told you how tight your pussy was, and gave you a back rub, doesn't mean he loves you, or understands you, or even wants you. Desire can be a tricky thing and easily mistaken for true love.

You still stand a chance of being one out of five because, for some men, it's not that deep. Throughout history, men have realized that it's compliments, attention, and special treatment that make a woman think she's the catch in less than a week. Let me not even get started on how men have figured out ways to manipulate themselves into a woman's body or heart without even deserving it, because women are often so quick to indulge in the satisfaction of being wanted and validated that they forget to ask themselves: What do I really expect from love? What do I want? What do you want? What do we want as human beings? At the end of the day, it doesn't even matter who you are or what gender you are. You get to determine what you need and what makes you happy.

Are you just deprived of love, or looking for love, or both? Are you simply longing for physical touch? It's okay to admit that you want love. We all do. It's human nature. It's what we need to evolve, not just as individuals, but as a species.

Well, whenever we get sloppy with our priorities and figuring out what we want without being clear, a lot of us learn the hard way. Because that same person we thought we loved, and who we thought loved us, wasn't there when life punched us in the face. When things got hard, they disappeared like ghosts, giving us lame excuses about some issues they were working through. It took me a while to realize that not everyone who claims to love you can truly show up for you, and that some of it is also not their responsibility, but yours. But eventually I did. When people want to do the things you ask them to, they do it. When they don't, they just don't. At this point, you have to understand what your deal breakers are.

I think you've noticed that I refer to all people in my life as X. I will never forget when X said to me, "I think I'm polyamorous and I want us to have an open relationship." I said, "Okay, let's do it." I'd never tried it and was open to experimenting. I don't judge, and I'm usually open to new things. I had one condition, though: safe sex at all times and honesty about who we slept with. One night, X and I lay cuddled up in bed, and he told me about this girl he had met. They had sex, but he claimed all he could think about was me. I didn't believe him, but kept it cute in the moment. After all, we were both artists. He was very charismatic and beautiful. I didn't blame the girl. I fell for X the moment I laid eyes on him. It would have been delusional of me to think that he wouldn't have the same effect on other women. When it was his turn to ask me what had happened, I hesitated for a moment. I had spent the night with a very handsome model I met at a fashion event. I looked up at the ceiling and told him. He wanted to know details about how we did it, and I openly shared my experience. X's energy changed almost instantly, and in a very dry, calm manner, he stated that he didn't want to be in an open relationship anymore. That was that, I guess.

Good sex is easy. Love is hard. It's challenging to really commit to someone, to show up for them even if it's not convenient for you. It's not fun to grow together. It is tedious work that results in a good amount of self-reflection and awareness. Long, sticky arguments, sleepless nights, heartache, and heartbreak. Good love is hard to achieve. They don't teach you about it in school. All the media does is bombard you with romance, the spectacle of love, and the façade of it all. And because most of us don't have the communication tools to stay in love, it's always easier to blame everyone else for our shortcomings and move on to the next. Real love, on the contrary, is not what they make you believe. It's far from romance. It means standing on business, keeping your side of the deal up, and working on yourself daily. That's why people fuck around and make everything about themselves, moving from person to person just to avoid one inch of accountability. It's simple. You don't have to integrate your spirit or deal with anyone's emotional baggage. You can go through life monkey-climbing from partner to partner, avoiding taking accountability for your actions and other people's feelings. Love takes guts. It takes skills and integrity. And throughout my life, I've discovered that most people have neither.

So, how do we learn what love actually is? There's no formula. No "10 Steps to Find Your Soulmate" bullshit. But I will say this: every asshole you meet is essential. Every heartbreak is a lesson. Every ugly fight, every messy breakup, every time you sat in your car crying after a fight and thought, "I'm never doing this again," it all matters. Love is shaped through the experience of finding out who you are and what you want from a potential partner because one day, you'll wake up, look at yourself, and realize you're over the despair and self-doubt. You are deserving of a love that serves you. That makes you happy. You're not afraid of love anymore. You're not numb to it either. You want to give it another shot. And that's when you've found yourself a little more. You're just you. And being you will attract those who are for you and those who aren't. You've heard that a million times, but have you actually internalized what it means?

Think about it. You can develop feelings for a stranger or someone you have known for a long time. Someone who had zero relevance to your existence five minutes ago, or someone you have overlooked your entire life. That's insane. That's beautiful. It's the irrational, chaotic luxury of being alive. To feel so deeply that you do ridiculous things, like cut your bangs at 2 a.m. or move to another country for someone you met on a dating app. Be proud of that. Don't run from those feelings. They're here to teach you something, and it's primarily serving to show you how to love yourself better. As much my past relationships were shit shows, I do not regret a single one of them. They all taught me to make better choices for myself and my health. I'm grateful to all my exes. In fact, I feel nothing but love for them because each and every one of them has one thing in common. They helped me become a better version of myself by being exactly who they are at that moment. I never stayed to please them. I always left to please myself.

Relationships aren't just about the other person. They're supposed to teach you how you want to be loved. In my opinion, you can never get it right when it comes to love. It's that one thing we can't foresee or control, and it sucks. Stop idolizing people who you think have a seemingly perfect relationship. They are not. Your number one task is to love yourself. Find someone who can help you by loving themselves enough to show up authentically. Be cautious; the relationship is doomed if one person doesn't value themselves. Is it filled with resentment, frustration, and bitterness? That's all just self-doubt masked as relationship problems. Make sure the person who claims to love you loves themselves more. Being around insecure, self-loathing people is bad for your health. It's a contagious self-harming vibration that will affect you if you are not careful.

We all love love. However, for some reason, most of us act as if admitting that is a kind of weakness. There is tackiness attached to admitting that you love love. Almost as if you didn't get the memo. Love hurts. It makes you vulnerable. That's inefficient when you are trying to be in control of your life and feelings, right? It's kind of embarrassing how much we care about love. But we do. So, let's keep going. Hear me out.

Content, music, movies, and novels have squeezed every drop out of the topic, and still, we sit here, wondering why this messy, chaotic, beautiful thing means so much to us. Maybe it's because love isn't logical. It's unpredictable and brutal. There is no script or manual on how to do and feel it successfully. It also doesn't help that we see love through our cracked, often delusional, personal, and distorted lenses. What feels like love to you might feel like codependency to someone else. What feels like passion to one person might feel like chaos to another. Love is personal and insanely intimate. But somehow, it's also universal. And that's my favorite part. It amazes me every time. No matter how different we are, no matter what languages we speak, what cultures we're from, and what trauma we carry, love is the common theme we keep pulling on. It's the thing we never get tired of exploring. It does something to us. And no matter how hard we try, we can't shake that it means everything and the world to everybody.

So what is the problem? We all have wildly different ideas of what love even is. Some people think love comes with flowers, long walks, poetry, movie nights, and others think it's tolerating someone's chewing sounds without committing murder. Some think love is a perfectly curated Instagram post with matching outfits and a caption like, "My person. My forever." Gross. Gives me the creeps. As much as I love love, I cringed so hard when I posted one of my wedding pictures on the gram. Like, who do I think I am to show off my commitment to the world? Just tacky. And in total despair, I had to watch how the most traction I ever gained on social media was because of my declaration of love. The common ground. The ultimate truth we all crave. Love, love, love.

No matter how different we are, whether you're a vegan yogi or a chain-smoking nihilist, love is the one thing we can't stop chasing. It's like a glitch in the human system. We need it. We want it. And we can't explain why.

AI doesn't have this problem. A computer doesn't need to be cuddled to function. You don't have to whisper sweet nothings to your laptop for it to turn on. It just works, unlike us. We fall apart without connection. Humans are messy and needy like that. We stumble through different stages of love, each more ridiculous than the last. We don't run on code. We run on Connection. Remember being a teenager? When love wasn't just an emotion but a life-threatening condition. Your heart raced if they liked your post. You practically had a cardiac event when they texted, "Goodnight :)." And God help you if they didn't. You'd lie awake at 3 a.m., staring at the ceiling, wondering why life was so cruel. Pathetic times but needed.

Fast forward to adulthood. You'd think we'd grow out of it. Spoiler: we don't. You still say dumb shit when you meet someone who blows your mind. You still lose sleep over people who don't text back. The stakes are higher now because you have bills to pay and no time to go nuts about somebody you just met. Or maybe you're in that "mature" love phase; the one where you've been with someone long enough to communicate telepathically from across the room. You don't even need words. You just know. And sure, they annoy the hell out of you sometimes, but they're your person, and you'd fight anyone who said otherwise. Clap, clap, clap.

Suppose you've felt any of this: congratulations. You're still human. You haven't turned into a robot. You still crave touch, desire, and connection. And no, that doesn't make you weak. It makes you alive. Now, let's take a deep breath. In. Out.

What the fuck are we supposed to do with all these feelings? Speaking about the System, these sentiments do not benefit capitalism. Unless on Valentine's Day, when everyone gets manipulated into buying trivial shit to prove their love. Are we really making it about the other person? Or is it all about us? Your first love story wasn't some teenage crush or that one situationship you still overthink. It was your parents. That was it. That was your first crash course in love. Good or bad, your childhood plays a significant role in how you choose to love or be loved by others. Whether they nailed it or fucked it up beyond recognition, that experience set the tone for how you love now. It's like a blueprint you didn't ask for but can't seem to shake. Careful. I'll never pretend to have all the answers. And let's be honest. Even people who grew up in picture-perfect homes can end up as emotional wrecks and sadistic mass murderers, so I don't know how tight my theory is. I can only speak for myself and based on my own experiences.

Every person you choose to love as an adult is a mirror. They reflect how you were taught to view love. Once you figure that out, you can start asking the real questions. I tended to pick men who were emotionally and physically absent, like my father. Those who doubted themselves and needed saving. To put it another way, we sometimes find comfort in what we are accustomed to, which can lead us to make poor decisions.

This is what I started asking myself. What do you actually want from love? Are you looking for someone to fix the holes your childhood left behind? Are you chasing people who remind you of home, even if "home" feels like walking on eggshells to ensure everyone else is okay, but you? It took me years to realize that the men I chose couldn't patch up the fact that my father failed me. And it took even longer to understand that watching my mother work herself into the ground made me believe I had to overproduce just to be lovable or feel worthy.

When someone stops caring for themselves and becomes overly dependent, controlling, or otherwise, it's a good idea to take a step back and reevaluate. Distance helps solve problems better than we admit it does. Love isn't about losing yourself in another person. It's about finding someone who helps you stay true to yourself. That's the kind of love worth evolving for. It takes time to develop, and it will be chaotic, challenging, and most of all, worth it.

My husband and I work on our marriage every single day. It's not always pretty, but it's always worth it. I value every confrontation and fallout, even when it gets ugly, because we always emerge from it stronger, clearer, and with a deeper understanding of who we are as individuals and what we expect from each other.

Marriage isn't for everyone, but I absolutely love being married. The commitment turns me on. The fact that we chose each other to do life with is an exquisite feeling, one I'll cherish forever.

The world needs more people who love love for what it truly is, a never-ending mystical interpretation of our emotional landscape. People who are not afraid to fight for it, even when it gets uncomfortable, even when it demands growth.

Chapter 15
Be Honest, but Not to People

As an artist, I observe myself with a certain distance. Like a stranger who's still a friend. I apply dry, ironic observations to my own behavior and draw quiet conclusions from them. That's what keeps things in perspective. I never wanted to become one of those tortured creatives who take themselves too seriously. Feeling light despite everything I've lived through, and maintaining a certain level of intentional superficiality in daily life, has always helped me stay grounded. I will always choose a kitchen dance over a serious conversation. I humbly state that this has been the key to my success. I explored that attitude in 2020 with my EP OBAA YAA, and again with the single What's Good, which dove even deeper into that mindset. Keeping it light, playful, and nonchalant is essential for progress. It means you're not held hostage by your own mind. And that's exactly how I see it.

Writing this book isn't about convincing you of my knowledge. I know that I know nothing, and that's essential in a world where most people make up their minds in two seconds, depending on what they've been told to believe. This book is a window into how I operate. How I feel things deeply without drowning in them. How do I stay open without getting walked over? When I write lyrics or create music, I slip into a dimension where no one is watching. It's intimate. Unfiltered. Sometimes raw, sometimes sarcastic, occasionally too complex to digest in one sitting. My music reflects whatever state my inner world is in; unpolished, honest, and always shifting.

That's not how I operate daily in real life. Not everyone needs to know what you know. Secrets are chic. There is a world where things do not have to be heard, seen, or discussed. There is beauty and power in not revealing the entire truth to people around you. Keep your guard up as long as it serves you. Be careful with how openly you share yourself with others. Mentally and physically. Mind you, it is essential to know yourself before others do. And that shifts constantly and takes time. Some people simply can't handle you in your entirety, and that's fine. That's not your problem to solve. Your job is to figure out just how much honesty the world around you can take. It's a skill. Trust me, not everyone is built for the truth. And most importantly: your truth. The balance between truth and tact is something only a few people understand. Let me try my best to break it down.

Unlike many people, I don't think you have to be an open book. Actually, the more vague you keep it, the better. Like a diary with quotes, with only a few crucial words written down, just enough to get the message across, but leaving plenty of room for interpretation. The more conversation about what you "meant," the better. There is a beauty in remaining vague to people who don't know you unless you want them to know you. But who wants anyone to know them entirely if it's not 5 years down the line?

Embrace your own mystery and make sure you only open up to the ones who can hold space for you entirely.

Share what you want, when you want, but only if you feel comfortable. And before you tell anyone, write it down. Why? Because it gives you a moment to hear how it sounds outside of your head. You don't want to go around blurting raw, unfiltered thoughts that trigger strong reactions. Not because you care what people think, but because there's no need to create unnecessary obstacles to getting what you want by scaring people off with your inner world. I believe in keeping it sweet, simple, and slightly superficial, especially in early encounters, and sometimes even beyond. Not everyone can handle the full expression of your mind, and they don't have to. Who cares if they get you? It's not their job to keep up. I'm a big fan of skilled small talk, polite compliments, and classy composure. Asking thoughtful questions is underrated these days, in a world where everyone seems obsessed with hearing themselves talk, online and offline.

Listening is way more powerful than talking. So why not start by listening to yourself more closely? It works wonders. You can even record yourself on your phone to hear the vibe you give off when saying certain things. I've used this technique countless times to prepare for business meetings, networking events, or interviews. I often hear people say, "I hate hearing my voice on recordings." But why? If you can't stand the sound of your own voice, why should anyone else enjoy listening to you?

The only person you owe complete honesty to is yourself. The rest of the world? Well, let's just say some folks are better off with a bit of fabrication here and there.

If you want to try being honest with someone you care about, try this: Start small. Tell someone they've gained a bit of weight, or drop a hint about what a mutual friend said behind their back. You'll learn quickly who can take it and who needs a gentle "oh, you're perfect just the way you are." How people handle the truth about themselves shows you a lot about how they will handle your truth. It's not about being cruel, it's about knowing your audience. Some people are like toddlers playing with a crystal ball. They're not built to carry the weight of the truth without dropping it and letting it fall into pieces.

Always remember that everyone wants to be real, authentic, and honest until they are not on the receiving end. People love artists because they are so "real," but they lose their shit when their friend tells them the truth about how they need therapy instead of a new relationship.

Insecure people love lies. Especially the lies they tell themselves about themselves. That they can't do anything, that they are not good enough. That they don't look good. It's a lie. But they told themselves that lie to a point where, when they are confronted with someone who refuses to put themselves down, it feels like an offence. Telling lies feels like oxygen to them. Ever wonder why they're so insecure in the first place? They've been fed so many lies that their self-worth is built on quicksand, from their parents' constant dishonest reassurance as a child up to their invented image of self. It's okay to tell children No. Or let them know when they haven't done the best job, and that they can do better.
It's not your job to constantly reassure your insecure friend unless you feel like playing emotional ping-pong. I tell you something nice, you tell me something nice. No, that's not how it works. The

people you trust and who are truly worthy of that trust should be able to listen to you like you are the universe, without projecting their insecurities or worldview onto you. And of course, you do the same in return. There are no middle grounds. Trust must be earned. It is a daily practice, a discipline. People like that are rare. If you have someone like that in your life, keep them. Protect them.

I also wouldn't recommend telling your heart to people who live on the scared and worried side of things. The so-called doom players. They lie like they breathe, spinning worst-case scenarios like a bad, cheap thriller. Let them. It's just their way of avoiding the fact that reality isn't nearly as scary as what they've made up in their heads, unless they were truly affected by war, catastrophe, or hunger. And if they have that much time to obsess over it, it probably means they're not affected at all. A prophet of doom cannot change the world for the better if they are not even capable of changing themselves.

Now, let's get this straight. Being a liar isn't the goal. You're not here to deceive people or ruin lives. That's the dark side of lying, and it will wreck you. Lying with bad intent is for losers, and you are not a loser. You are brave, and you live in your truth. Being dishonest with the intention to harm others messes with your head and your body. Your nervous system takes the hit. Even if no one else catches you, you'll live with the fear of being found out. It's like a horror movie that never ends, dread lurking around every corner, the moment you close your eyes at night. You don't need that kind of stress. Instead, lie to yourself in a constructive, positive way. Lie to yourself beautifully. I tell myself every morning that I'm the healthiest woman in the world. Do I believe it every day? No. Would other people believe me if I said it out loud? Also no. But who cares? It doesn't have to be true for it to feel good. And let me tell you, feeling good and healthy is worth everything. It is a powerful, magical feeling that you should not miss out on.

Sometimes, you just need to be a little delusional. Not too much, keep it at a solid 50/50. Dream big, aim high, trip over yourself, roll around in the dirt, and then do it all over again. Being grounded and rational at all times is overrated. The world already has enough people keeping both feet on the ground, making decisions rooted in worry, fear, and negativity. We need more people willing to float into the clouds, chasing wild, impossible ideas that make life enjoyable. Be delusional, but not entirely. Know when to tell the truth, when to stretch it, and when to keep your mouth shut altogether. And most importantly, don't forget to tell yourself the kind of beautiful lies that keep you dreaming and aspiring for positive outcomes.

The world needs more people who guard their truth like a treasure, who choose silence not out of fear but power, and who tell themselves beautiful lies until their reality catches up.

Chapter 16
Money Does NOT Rule the World,
and You Always Knew That

My mother never had much money, but she had wild ideas. Ideas that carried more value than any overflowing bank account. Ideas that shaped me and my life in the most positive ways. Not only did she pay for all my piano and dance classes while working so much that, in hindsight, I don't know how she did it, but she also made the decision early on to show me the world, or at least the parts of it that mattered to her. We saw Europe one capital at a time, riding second-rate buses with Rainbow Tours because it was the cheapest option. She booked us into the shabbiest hotel in Pigalle, a place so grim we made a sport of staying out all day just to avoid it.

Still, there we were, mother and daughter, eating a baguette while walking, laughing in the streets of Paris. I had watched Moulin Rouge five times by then, and when we climbed the steps of Montmartre, I looked out over the city and quietly swore: I'll live here one day. I was 12. It wasn't the hotel or the money we didn't have; it was the feeling. The dream.

The art of making something out of absolutely nothing. Escaping the stress at home, determined to live life to the fullest. What mattered was not what we lacked, but what we imagined. We had problems, yes. But in that moment, we also had Paris. And that was more than enough. She took me to London as well, and after she took a picture of me on London Bridge, I ran into her arms, almost yelling: Mama, I'll live here one day. I've lived in Paris as an adult, and I'm currently living in London. As I'm writing this, I can't hold back my tears. I'm grateful for life, but most of all, I'm grateful for my mother. With everything she went through in her relationship with my father, she curated these moments for us. A true hero. As I've gotten older, I make a habit of letting her know how impressed I am with her bravery. She made mistakes, yes. She could have left earlier, yes, to that too. But she did her best, and I'm proud of her for making it through to the other side. She was way over 50 when she had her first therapy session. Since then, we haven't stopped talking about what we've been through together. Sometimes it's easy, sometimes it's hard. But it's always helpful to talk about it.

Every now and then, you've got to shut off the scarcity script in your brain, that endless loop telling you that you need more. More money, more things, more proof of your worth. It's exhausting. It ages you. It carves permanent worry lines into your face, the kind that scream: I'm safe, fed, clothed, and still unsatisfied. With all the stress my mother was going through, she still understood the importance of showing me the world, making time for me, buying me books, and paying for my music lessons. Catch yourself. Ask: What do I have? What can I see, taste, build, or become? Sometimes the answer isn't in owning more, but in doing something unexpected, like doing something nice for yourself, even when you feel broke and think you shouldn't. That's what we did. And that's why I still believe that having the best ideas will always be richer than having the most money.

Money is a made-up transaction medium created by mankind to create order and differentiate classes. Its history is deeply linked to exchange and value. What do we put between ourselves and what we have to offer? How do we regulate and separate ourselves to keep structures and hierarchy going? Through money. Humans define the price of goods, not the money itself. It is essential to understand that before you even think about wanting to make money. Money itself holds no value. You can't eat money, you can't hug or make love to money, you can't use money to keep yourself safe from a natural catastrophe or a wild animal. However, money can facilitate means to keep you safe from many things, make people love and respect you, and buy you food that keeps you nourished and healthy. Understanding this is key. It is not the money that rules the world, but our relationship and perspective on it.

To make money means to create money. There is an artistic approach to creating value and pricing that is truly underestimated. Your ability to make money is deeply linked to your attitude toward money. If you grew up never lacking anything, your relationship to money will differ from someone who constantly heard their parents fight about it. What are your conditioned thoughts attached to money? If you grew up never worrying about it, your relationship with it will be worlds apart from someone who watched their parents argue over bills. Poverty has a way of passing itself down, not through some curse, but through inherited attitudes. And that mindset is crucial when it comes to creating or being of value in this world. A poverty mindset is a way of thinking in which someone believes they'll never have enough money or resources, no matter what they do. People with this mindset often focus on scarcity, and greed and fear become their guiding spirits. They fear losing whatever they have, whether a lot or a little. They avoid taking risks or investing in opportunities that could improve their situation because of the voice in their head that tells them it's not going to work. They might also feel stuck or undeserving of financial success, which can hold them back from growing or changing their circumstances. The feeling of not being worthy hinders the creation and manifestation of value. The feeling of not wanting to lose what you have creates losing what you have and what you could have.

Importantly, how much are we willing to pay for things we need or that make us happy? All prices are made up. Tomatoes grow on vines, apples grow on trees, but the structure around them creates the value of money. I never worship or want money. My relationship with money is determined by how I see myself and the value I put on things. Understanding that my creative approach to life is what is going to make me money, correction, has made me money, changed everything. If you are a corporate baddie deciding to get hired for a job that pays you well, you don't hope to get hired; you know you will be hired because you know you are worth the opportunity. And if it doesn't turn out to be that job, it will be another one, because you are convinced that who or what rejects you has nothing to do with the bigger picture and vision of yourself. Don't get it twisted. The richest woman can still be held captive by her mind, thinking that nothing is ever good enough, hoarding all she has, and rarely being generous out of fear that she might not have enough for herself. This creates a cycle of unhappiness and bad fortune. You will only receive what you are ready to give. Not more and not less.

Like it or not, your relationship with money is directly tied to your self-esteem. Why do you think a lot of very wealthy people almost come across as narcissistic and delusional, and obsessed when it comes to their ideas and concepts? There is no lie. People who love making money love themselves in a very disciplined, persistent, odd way, to a point where they could be broke, living in their friend's basement, sleeping on a gym mat. They would still pursue their dreams with conviction and determination, not feeling too good to sleep on the floor.

If you've always had what you needed, money might not carry the same weight for you as it does for someone raised in scarcity, watching their family stretch pennies and survive on resilience alone. Poverty is not only material, it is psychological. It seeps into the stories we inherit, into what we believe we deserve, and into how we imagine our capacity to thrive. We often speak of money as a numbers game, but more than anything, it's a reflection of self-perception. If you fear judgment more than you trust your potential, you will shrink yourself into roles that barely sustain you. And if you quietly believe you are worth little, the world will meet you at that price. It isn't arrogance to know your value. Everything you offer, every gesture, every decision, is a mirror of that belief. The world responds not to your hustle, but to your internal permission to receive. Regardless of where they come from, people who feel deserving of success often tend to achieve it magically. Disposable wealth, houses, cars, and endless means do not define success. Your happiness and satisfaction are a direct translation of your success. We don't need more paranoid, miserable, greedy rich people. We need more people who link success to purpose and vice versa, and who know that giving back is the real luxury.

Not everyone is destined to be an entrepreneur, and that's not a flaw. Too often, self-worth is confused with being at the top of some imagined pyramid, when in truth, it lies in recognizing the value of what you already do. Whether you're a teacher, a cleaner, a doctor, or a carpenter, your worth is not determined by a title or flashy ventures. Despite what the tech prophets preach, these professions are sacred, and no machine will ever fully replace the emotional depth of human presence. People will always pay for joy, comfort, and care. There is a quiet luxury in not needing to cut costs by replacing humans with computers, especially in places like hospitals and schools. Never underestimate your craft. Thinking small of yourself won't raise your income; becoming excellent at what you do will. That's why the get-rich-quick cult of YouTube gurus in borrowed Ferraris is so corrosive. They sell a fantasy and skip the truth: true wealth begins with knowing your value. Most haven't built a thing. They inherited their comfort, dressed it up as hustle, and now monetize your insecurities with recycled clichés. In reality, making money isn't just about grinding; it's about believing you're worth the effort. It's taking bold risks, investing in your growth, and developing the discipline to carry your ambition. Yes, luck plays a part, and yes, generational wealth can open doors. But for the rest of us, it starts with one undeniable truth: money comes from creating value, and you are the source of that value. You. You. You.

Don't be intimidated by those who have more. Most wealthy people either inherited their status or crossed lines you might never want to cross. There is no magic formula. You are a beautiful human being with your own compass, unimpressed by wealth alone. You connect with people because they bring value to your life, because they are kind, intelligent, and grounded, not because of their bank account. People are always dishonest about where their money comes from because they are trying to protect it. Don't believe what these YouTubers tell you. Create a mindset of self-esteem and learn a skill that makes you unique. The world doesn't just need nurses. It needs kind, funny nurses for all areas. Some are good around kids, and others are good around disabled people. All these things hold incredible value. I also do not believe in feeling sorry for people who have less than you. That's just condescending. I respect people for who they are and where they are financially and being rich or poor does not make you better or worse. Deciding to help is different because you think people who might not have the means to progress are essential. That's not because you feel sorry for them, but because you see the worth in what they are doing and think it's crucial to elevate their course.

Walk through a world where you decide what is worth your money. Do you need to eat out every day or impress your friends with a certain car or outfit? Is your business idea still not taking off after five years? Maybe it's time to rethink and restructure. If you feel underpaid, unite with your colleagues and appeal to your boss. Is the gym too expensive? Meet in the park. Don't walk into your job like a ghost; walk in like you're about to conquer the world. Change it or change your attitude toward it. One of my favorite cities in the world is New York, where the energy is electric and the mindset magnetic. You can feel what it means to create wealth just by how people move. Their positive, upbeat attitude, their excellence in execution, no matter the job, and their unity when it comes to fighting for a cause. It's breathtaking.

One of the main reasons certain countries lack stability and resources is not because they lack money. They lack vision, unity, and fairness. Having spent a significant amount of time in West Africa, I have seen with my own eyes how a government that does not value its own people and wages economic wars against the poorest of the poorest leaves people hopeless and exhausted. Yes, we do have to consider the unfairness of exploitation and the consequences of colonization. Still, working and living in these countries, I realized that a lot of the damage is caused by greed and a lack of good governance that prioritizes the country's people.

My view on money has been critical since I understood how deeply it is linked to mindset and mentality. You cannot build a healthy economy around people who are deeply unhappy and painfully aware of their limitations. You must first provide education that teaches them their worth. I urge you to invest in yourself before considering investing in stock. You will earn as much as you believe you deserve, and that belief is reflected in how much time, energy, and love you put into your work and into yourself. Creating money is a beautiful act when you learn to see it that way. The next time you earn something, spend it on something that brings you joy. Then spend something on someone else, and let that generosity build an energy that welcomes more. Stay calm when you are losing money. Treat it like a flow, sometimes steady, sometimes thin, but always returning, especially when your energy around it is rooted in peace rather than fear.

The world needs more people who are impressed by art, culture, and nature, not by possessions, but by the real value they bring to life.

Chapter 17
Why You Care

True confidence is something I acquired way later in life. That feeling of being completely okay in your body and at ease with your mind, and after that, combining and reuniting the two to come back to self. Being unforgiving about who you are and feeling no shame for your flaws and shortcomings. I would say that feeling only kicked in around my mid-thirties.

One of the main reasons I self-harmed in my mid to late twenties was not because I hated myself. It was because I wanted to love myself and felt guilty every time I did. Feeling like the gifts and blessings you're being showered with aren't meant for you is disturbing, self-destructive, and confusing. Even though I knew I had worked hard for my success, there was something inside me that felt guilty about not being able to enjoy it. I dressed up. I performed. I travelled the world, only to come back to my apartment, shut the blinds, overeat, throw up, and then take out my favorite pink lighter. It was a sacred ritual. I'd mostly sit on the floor, leaning against the wall, fully aware I was doing something that wasn't normal, something that would leave scars. Something people would ask me about. My left wrist was my preferred area because I could control the flame with my right hand. I'd roll up my sleeve and start by flicking the lighter. The sound felt comforting. I would then hold the flame up to my skin and slowly watch the color change. It took about five seconds before I felt anything. Then the pain would kick in. A pain I could locate, understand, and contextualize. Pain, I was grateful for because I knew where it came from. I was in control of it. I could see and feel my wounds afterward because they were physical instead of emotional. I sometimes used the same wound because I didn't want to have too many scars, and the fresh wounds hurt more than the new skin I would burn. Yes, I actively sought out pain to distract myself from what was actually going on; a deep emotional wound festering in my soul and spirit. Wounds no one could see. Wounds no one could assist me with. I loved this process. After I was done, I would just sit there, numb and exhausted. It was the greatest feeling of all. I would nurse my wounds depending on how bad they were, take two sleeping pills, and sleep for 12 to 14 hours. This was my way of creating balance and context for what I was feeling on the inside. And when people asked what happened to my wrist, I said, "Oh, you know, I took something out of the oven and burned myself. Silly me." I used my oven for storage. Everyone who knew me knew that. Everyone who knew me knew I was self-harming, but chose not to speak about it. I think that's okay. I think they were right, because what could they have possibly said to me?

Let's talk about confidence, which is rooted in the type of self-acceptance that is guilt-free and bold. I've always disliked the assumption that confidence means strutting around like a peacock, pretending nothing touches you, that you're somehow floating above the chaos of life, bulletproof and untouchable. Please. If that's your definition of confidence, you've confused repression with strength. True self-worth is not a performance. It doesn't require a stage, a spotlight, or a rehearsed monologue about how perfect your life is. It's not found in your six-pack, your LinkedIn summary, or your ability to keep a stiff upper lip while everything inside you is quietly cracking.

Let me put it simply. No one, and I mean no one, is consistently strong, positive, successful, and carefree. The people who try to convince you they are? Be cautious. They are the ones most likely to snap. I no longer trust anyone who cannot admit they are having a bad day. That kind of emotional constipation is not noble. It is dangerous. We are now swimming in an ocean of digital dopamine dealers, life coaches, influencers, and gurus, all screaming the same slogan: optimize, improve, hustle, smile. As if breathing deeply enough and journaling hard enough will guarantee you a life without suffering. Bullshit.

Life is wonderful, but sometimes it's awful. You'll disappoint people. You'll disappoint yourself. You'll say the wrong thing, hurt the right person, sabotage something good just because you didn't know better. That's part of it. It's called being human. You can either spend your life trying to curate a flawless personality or you can relax, accept your contradictions, and focus on becoming someone real.

The most powerful people I've met don't flex. They're calm, curious, and more interested in asking questions than telling stories about themselves. And when they speak, it's never to prove their worth, it's to open their mind to something new. That, to me, is real confidence. It is the ability to sit with your discomfort and not panic. It is choosing to solve your problem instead of performing it. It is the strength of saying, "This isn't working for me," and taking action without needing a round of applause or extra motivation.

I've met people, sharp, layered, brilliant women, who radiate that kind of energy. Not because they're perfect, but because they've made peace with their imperfections. They don't spiral into self-doubt every time they make a mistake. They don't rely on external validation to feel whole. They focus on what brings them joy, and they let the rest fall away. We're all quick to identify what's wrong. But how fast are we to seek a solution? How honest are we willing to be with ourselves? Sometimes confidence is just five quiet minutes alone, acknowledging how far you've come, even if the world never applauds you for it. Sometimes it's being able to say, "I'm okay" and actually mean it, even if nothing looks particularly impressive on paper. You don't need to be amazing all the time. You don't need to prove anything. You just need to be honest, stay curious, and take responsibility for your energy.

Confidence means caring. Caring for yourself and your community. You can only change what you change within. You can only heal what you heal within. There is no fancy way to word this. Here is why you should care. You should care because a siren is going off inside you, screaming and yelling: I want to grow. Stagnant energy doesn't fulfill you. I can tell by the way you are constantly looking for the next fix, the way you won't stop searching, the way you never think you are outstanding enough, and the way you keep looking for love even though you claim you're not. By the way, you keep improving and feel shitty when someone's way more relevant than you. Oh, that's not you? You've got it all figured out? Yeah okay. You are far from perfect, and that's the way it should be. All you have left is to make it look seemingly perfect and hope they don't notice the human ball of cell reproduction and reduction you are. A bunch of DNA intertwined and mashed up. Someone who can only exist because someone before them existed, offspring of offspring of offspring. You've come a long way from feeling like something is off, and yes, there surely is. You are human. And we live in an ever-changing world where there will always be something off.

True freedom and confidence are found in accepting your God-given human defects instead of rejecting them. You think they still haven't noticed that you pretend most of the time? Do you only tell them about the good things? Do you never show your vulnerability because you feel like some people might use it against you? Nothing lasts forever. No thing on this planet, and you, my love, are one of those things. When will you feel thankful for this unique opportunity to leave your mark? When will you stop complaining and worrying about every single fucking thing? When will you shut up, be quiet, and start talking with your breaths? Oxygen is all your anxiety needs, dear friend. Your body is craving proper blood circulation, so go stand on your head or something. I always feel like I'm eating the nut's brain when I'm cracking open pistachios or walnuts. And I sometimes become my own brain-eater while being convinced that I'm going nuts. That's insane. That's called being normal.

Problems can easily turn into your holy grail. Your brain creates them and strongly reacts to them because it wants to find solutions, solutions that create new realities, positive ones and negative ones, depending on what you feel within. How fucking fragile can our human race be? Very fragile, for we mainly act on impulse and emotion, even when we've studied in universities and read Kafka from front to back. The human mind is by far the most complex organ. We maneuver through life, taking for granted the years and years of cerebral evolution. What do we even know? I'm not even sure if what we say we know is what we really know. The first evidence of humans creating and using fire dates back 1 to 1.5 million years ago. The half-ape, half-human who had the privilege of discovering fire must have thought about what miracle unfolded before them. Or did they think at all? Did she know it was possible? Did he know about it before he tried it? Did she follow her intuition? Was it a he or a she? Does it matter? Well, no. Because now we can't even go an hour without checking our phones. Evolution moves quicker than our brains because it's the collective consciousness of who we are that wants to evolve.

Now, back to us. Back to you. It's okay to care about your environment and for yourself. True confidence requires care instead of nonchalance. That's healthy. Because you feel strongly about the world, she has gotten to you for some reason. You feel emotionally attached to her because you've realized you need her. You know that you are dependent on her, and she is not reliant on you. So, deep down, we as a human race realize we have to self-correct after a billion years of chaos if we want to keep her on our side. And the more dramatic thing is, she might not care. She will rotate, shift, evolve, throw up, reconstruct, break open, and eventually leave us for dust. Because she fucking can. She is the world, the queen, our life giver. She is the boss. Planet Earth and the little we know of her. I've always wondered where humans acquired the audacity of knowing better and best. So far, we've done a pretty shitty job at sustaining the only thing that nurtures us, the Earth, and our love and respect for it, disregarding that we are the problem.

I hope that answers your question about why you should care. Care about how you feel. Care about who you love. Care about nature. That's real confidence. Care about what nurtures you. Chances are you won't succeed, and the world will swallow you like the insignificant parasite we all are. That's why living your life with a little more intention and dedication is not just advised, it's urgent. And if you truly don't care about anything other than yourself, then at least make sure you never stop evolving. Tell yourself you are creating a more peaceful reality from the inside out so you can nourish what you involuntarily destroy just by being alive.

The world needs more people who care deeply and move through life with grounded, unwavering confidence.

Chapter 18
Fight Back, It's All You've Got for Now

The day I started fighting back was the day I felt autonomy over my spirit. Confronting my father about the continuous domestic violence and the emotional abuse I endured as a child and teenager was almost impossible, the shouting, the insults, the fury in his eyes. The constant accusation of making this all up in my head deeply disappointed me. How could such a brilliant artist, whose brain and intellect I admired to the core, be so volatile and incapable of self-reflection? The day he screamed at me, chasing me out of the house, yelling, he wished I'd never been born and that he should have ejaculated into the gutters instead of my mother, was the day my heart shattered into pieces that scattered across the universe. I've never been able to put it back together. It was the combination of the shouting, the vulgarity, and pure evil while throwing me out of my childhood home. How could anyone say that to their child? It remains the worst thing anyone has ever said to me, and it came from someone I repeatedly chose to love and forgive.

It was that day I decided to stop speaking to him. I wouldn't say forever, because if he ever came to me with honest self-reflection and a sincere apology, I'd be open to a conversation. If I had invited and accepted this type of disrespect in my own family, then there would be very little hope for me to attract healthy relationships that nourished me. We attract what we surround ourselves with because everything is energy. When we are constantly tuned into misery, heartbreak, and fear, then that's exactly what we receive.

Love is a tricky little big thing, because despite everything he said to me on that day, I still feel love for him. I love him only like a daughter can love her creator, her father. I've incorporated the love I feel for him into my work. He gave me the gift of music, culture, and heritage, and I give my daily best to be a messenger. Deep down, I know he loves me too. I also know he is proud of me. I still feel it, through every single sticky fallout. Even in the cruelest things he's ever said, I can still hear and feel his love for me.

A lot of times, letting shit go and being the bigger person is important. You decide when to apply it and when not. In my case, I'm not ready to tap into my higher self. Not today, maybe tomorrow, maybe never, maybe forever. Forgiveness does not require reunion. Those two things do not have to be linear. I permit myself to move in my own time.

Now let's talk about you. You don't need to be cool when you are angry; you also, depending on the setting, do not need to be an adult. Feel that anger rush through you as they say something inappropriate, or that man with his big gut, bald head, and dandruff on his shoulder tries to make a move on you, just to degrade and objectify you the moment he feels rejected. Send that red pill man to hell. How could they make a move on you? Turn around and call them a prick because that's precisely what they are- A huge ugly knob with the audacity to step to you. Nothing feels better than marking your territory. Piss against your tree baby.

How dare they not behave in your presence? All queens and kings fought dirty. Many wars are being fought between greatness and legacy. Most of them are bloody and brutal. We sometimes have to fight to regain our dignity, and it's not always pretty or classy.

I once remember proposing to a girlfriend whose partner had put his hands on her to slap the shit out of him with a spatula or poison him in his sleep. No, we are good people, we do not kill other human beings unless we are fighting for our lives. At least a laxative. One of those strong ones that makes you poop for 40 days and nights. Fight back when someone makes you feel like you are less. You are a whole galaxy, darling. Take your power back.

We had a boy in our school. He was not in my class, but he was in my crew. We all knew he was gay, and yes, I fought for him. You were not allowed to bully my friend. Worth it and not a single waste of my energy.

Science focuses on the measurable and observable, but the soul can't be explained or measured. We can't see or touch it, yet we confidently say something "touches our soul." It's like when you taste something so good you want to eat it over and over again. Or a kiss in the tropical rain, and the whole thing feels so ridiculously beautiful you want to cry. So you do, and then you taste the rain, the tears, and his lips. And this is how you always imagined it. Him, the kiss, the rain. Was your soul touched? Or a baby bunny that needs to be rescued, and you do it. You rescue it. Your soul is touched. You feel happy and vital.

We've reached a point where protecting our souls is no longer negotiable. It's not functional, not built from codes or formulas, or is it? What are our souls made of?

I feel like it's a phenomenon science still can't fully grasp. The soul is one of the few things that can't be programmed. It is wild and free if it wants to be. It's most likely spiritual, an undeniable force. The stronger our soul, the less power others have to manipulate or distort our reality. When you have decided you are great, beautiful, healed, and essential to the world, don't let anyone tell you otherwise. Not even your father. And when your mother tries to convince you to get a regular job because this 'artist' life is not going to pay your bills, lie to her. Tell her you will get a regular job, continue eating cornflakes all week, and attend that audition. And if you don't get picked at that audition, tell the jury to suck dick. Whisper it. Some things sound cooler when you whisper them. Go Suck Dick Ladies and Gentlemen. In a world of broken and obeyed laws, we often lean on something more profound than morals. Like knowing, deep down, it's wrong to kill another person or an innocent animal. Yet it happens constantly. Humanity has mastered justifying horrific actions while still finding a reason for them. We can't trust each other, yet we have to, so we can continue to exist.

I often equate the soul to a deep, underlying feeling that we all have; a heightened awareness of being alive. It's like a compass, guiding us toward heaven or hell on earth. It drives us to wake up every morning and search for whatever we've decided is worth living or not living for. But what do I know? I have limited time left to figure it all out. I'm 38 as I'm writing this. It is tragic. Time goes by quickly. I feel like an hourglass with sand on both sides. Still.

When something feels off, our soul senses it before our brain catches up. When someone bullies you, stand up for yourself. Do NOT be the bigger person in that case. I've never fully agreed with that. The bigger person for what? I do not let bullies win because they thrive on your loss. Either losing your shit or your composure. That's where I begin. I will twist your little joke into an even bigger joke. I'll make fun of you, call you an ass crumb, and ask you when you last had your prostate checked. For that reason, no one bullies me or used to bully me because they were not sure what would come back. I'm somewhat unpredictable but also very sweet and kind. Best to stay away from me or get really close to me.

Release yourself from the idea of wrong or right; the lines are blurred. All you can focus on is how you feel in the moment you're faced with choices. Do I stand up, or do I fold? Do I fight back or accept my fate? No one is supposed to make you feel uncomfortable. No one. And if they do, let them burn in a box. Symbolically, of course.

We all know that feeling when something's off, whether it's in our gut, tense muscles, or a sense of irritation. However we describe it, we recognize it without being able to see or touch it. That's the very thing we have to protect, because once we don't, we become emotional zombies, people who disregard their soul and hurt others to avoid feeling their own pain.

Until we fully understand the importance of speaking up for ourselves at all costs, the cycle of suffering won't end. So, do we stay silent to keep the peace, or fight back to protect our souls? The line between right and wrong has always been blurred, and the world won't make it easier for us to see. It's not about playing by someone else's rules or being the "bigger person." It's about defending that gut feeling, that unshakable awareness deep within. The moment we let it slip, we become victims, disconnected, hurting, and spreading that hurt to others.

There will be no inner peace without a battlefield. Know when it's time for love and when it's time for war. The world needs more people who are brave enough to face themselves.

Chapter 19
Solitude is for You

Solitude is an art form. You either learn to master it or let it consume you. I've always known that. Maybe it came more easily to me because I'm an only child and naturally drawn to being alone. Was I the kid who stood by herself at school? Absolutely. I stood there, arms crossed, staring down the others for not having the sense to come over. In my head, I was clearly the one with the best ideas and the most original hairstyle. I'm obviously being sarcastic here. There was always another kid who got the attention because they had the right backpack or wore pigtails with Sailor Moon ribbons. Sailor Moon was untouchable. I didn't have the ribbons, but I was convinced I embodied her. That's how expansive my imagination was, and still is. I never told anyone, of course. Why would I? Adults were experts in crushing dreams, and kids were known to steal ideas. I learned early on that solitude was not a weakness but a secret space where power, fantasy, and truth could live undisturbed.

I have never been afraid to stand alone. At a bar, at a party, in a gallery. Just like in school, I still question the herds that never seem to part ways, always orbiting a designated leader who decides what's funny, what's cool and what's not. Sometimes, I place myself inside these groups for the sake of curiosity. To feel what it's like to lose a little autonomy and float with the tide of social choreography. Not terrible. Surprisingly pleasant, in moderation. You just don't have to think for yourself that much. Groups serve their purpose. They teach us about human nature and how people behave when they think no one's really watching. I love observing people in all their contradictory glory. How generous of everyone to act out their carefully curated chaos in public. Most are desperate to be the main character. It is rare and almost sacred when someone stops and says, "And how have you really been?" It almost feels intimate.

Sometimes it doesn't matter how many people are around us. We still feel lonely. Singled out by the universe. Unable to relate. Unable to get a word in. No big deal. We are all alike and here to engage with the world. Most crucially with ourselves. I won't tire of pointing that out to you. You must be brave enough to stand alone until it feels awkward. It strengthens your character. Now, if you are always alone and your favorite place on earth is your sofa, stuffy bedroom, or garden, and all you do is talk to plants and send memes to friends you could actually reach out to, I'd suggest you try standing naked in the road for a few minutes to feel the breeze on your tits. Life is for living and learning. How will you expand your horizon if you are curled up in the house all day? Some people don't want to learn. They do not find joy in knowing there is more out there. That's fine too. But I find it suspicious and stay away when I see or feel tendencies like that creeping up inside me.

Yes, I stay away from things I don't like within myself, but only after fully confronting them and being aware of them.

That is the beauty of knowing yourself. You can be around your partner, your family, your kids constantly, but I would like to carefully toss into the room that your family is not a substitute for long-term personal growth. Comfort is not the same as evolution. If your idea of connection is sitting on the couch watching movies every night with your loved one, ask yourself, really, every single night? Why?

A big solution to figuring out what we want in life and who we are is spending time with ourselves, whether we find it uncomfortable or not. Get out and feel self-conscious. Leave your partner at home and don't tell them when you'll be back. Make new friends or ring your neighbor's bell and say hi. Sign up for a workshop or something. Go mingle. For God's sake, connect with the world — it was made for you. Communication is a dying skill, and it's because people sit in their houses on their phones, surrounded by the same people, for way too long. Get out or become weird. And not the cool, edgy type of weird. The creepy neighbor type of weird who never leaves the house.

To those who feel uncomfortable being alone, start telling people no. No, you can't come over. No, I'm not going out tonight. In fact, befriend the loner who never wants to meet up and get to work with your inner dialogue. Try journaling or singing out loud while cleaning the kitchen you've ignored for weeks because you were too busy having five picnics in the park last week, thanks to the great weather.

Some people drain you without saying much. You leave the conversation tired, irritable, and unsure why.

That's your sign. Energy vampires often cloak themselves in crisis and charm, but they leave behind a residue of fatigue, confusion, and self-doubt. Energy is contagious. If you are constantly surrounded by anxious people, you will start feeling some of the energy yourself. You won't always recognize them at first. They show up as colleagues, lovers, even family. But pay attention to how your nervous system responds when they enter the room. That's where the truth lives. Feel it. Feel your body at all times when you are around certain people.

Choose solitude over people who drain you. It sharpens you. It tunes your inner frequency before anyone else gets a chance to touch the dial. Find your rhythm. Prioritize yourself ruthlessly. Only then will you know what you actually need from the world and what it needs from you.

The world needs more people who are not afraid of being alone with themselves.

Chapter 20
Stay Clean

When I went through a period of chronic illness, it wasn't the sleepless nights, the fevers, or the endless hours tied to my bed that got to me. It was the fact that I couldn't get dressed up or do my makeup. Let's not even talk about hair. I love getting my hair done; it's the ultimate expression of my well-being. There is nothing more potent than tending to the crown of your brain. It was hell for me, and I developed an immense amount of empathy for people battling illness in hospitals or at home. Every trip to the bathroom felt like torture. I remember forcing myself to shower every single day, sometimes even twice, even though I was just lying in my clean sheets all day. It was about dignity and hygiene for me. It simply made me feel better to smell the soap. Organic soap course. None of the chemical harsh stuff they keep selling to us, trying to poison us instead of nourishing us. I urge you always to use clean products and be aware of what you allow close to your body. Do your research and download one of these cute apps that check the ingredients of each product you buy and use on your body. It's wild how the products designed to make us feel fresh and sexy are actually fucking with our hormones. The clean girl aesthetic doesn't mean much if your armpits are soaking up hormone disruptors and your skin's fighting a chemical war every time you shower. The damage isn't just surface-level; it gets deep, affecting everything from your mood to your metabolism. So let's get to work, but let's focus on using products that do not harm us.

Your head is a significant body part. Your face, your brain, your eyes, your mouth... your entire perception of the world runs through that space and gets processed up there. So why not take care of the one thing that decorates it the most? Your hair. Even if you've got short hair, a fresh buzz cut, and a healthy scalp, it looks super cute. Healthy, beautiful hair is one of the most significant indicators of physical well-being, regardless of what's happening in your bank account. The same goes for skin. Even if you've got acne, eczema, or a few scars, seeing someone take care of themselves without trying to cover it all up is hot. Yes, acne-prone skin can look clean and healthy, too. A little gloss on your lips, cute brows, and lashes that don't look neglected make a difference.

You'll never get it perfectly right, but that's not the point. If you are a man, make sure you have clean nails, fresh breath, and moisturized skin. You know the deal. The goal is to maximize hygiene and optimize your God-given features. Never underestimate the impact that a little cleanup can have on your mood and well-being. Grooming yourself, showering, moisturizing, fixing your hair, and choosing an outfit like it is battle armor is a ritual. And humans are weirdly devoted to it. We spend hours and money making ourselves a little more magnetic. A little more look at me, but don't look too hard. So, who is it really for?

Ourselves? Maybe. But also... perhaps we're just a bunch of birds, flashing our feathers, hoping someone says, "Damn. That's a nice one."

Grooming yourself is excellent for your mental health. Not because it'll fix your life, it won't, but because smelling excellent while everything is falling apart is a form of self-respect. You can't control the economy, your ex, or the government. But you can control whether or not you have deodorant on. Not the toxic one that clogs up your armpits, because not smelling like life is difficult, counts for something. Trust me. When I was ill, I learnt the hard way. Self-care is closely linked to dignity. No matter how hot you are, nature is hotter. The ocean? Hot. A thunderstorm? Sexy. The sunset? Literally perfect. But never when the oceans are polluted and the air is full of pollution. And I know it's difficult sometimes, when you are sick or depressed, but that's not the point. The point is to try anyway. Keep yourself clean. Smell good. Use soap under your feet, yes, under your feet. And between your toes. Get in there. And please, for the love of humanity, wash your ass. With soap. Not just a splash of water and a hand. This is not a fairy pond. You are a full-grown human being with a full-blown digestive system and the responsibility to keep your ass clean. There is something deeply poetic about a beautiful, clean bum.

You may not be as perfect as Mother Nature, but you can at least smell like you have respect for her. Before I forget, clean your house. Keep it clean at all times. You are old enough. You've got this.

The world needs fewer opinions and more rituals, rituals for self-care, self-respect, and the kind of hygiene that cleans both your body and your mind.

Chapter 21
Eat, Move, and Repeat

I've trained myself to keep moving. I hold a diploma in dance instruction and movement theory from a respected institute in contemporary dance. Studying anatomy, physiology, and the mechanics of movement for three years taught me how to hold myself accountable for my actions. I am my body, and my body is me. The brain is not a separate command center; it is part of every motion, every moment.

I've cultivated the habit of staying on track. I move to shut the noise up. I move to stay present, not perfect. I don't move to impress anyone. I move to stay sane. Even when I feel off, especially when I feel off, I move. The body always knows. The mind takes longer to catch up. Movement has a lot to do with feeling the momentum, being in the moment, but in motion. Our bodies want to be moved around in the hope that we begin to feel what is good for us. Veins, muscles, tissue, organs; all of it is waiting to be tended to.

There are moments when we wait for things to change. But how can anything shift when we don't move? Change requires momentum. New direction. A different position in space. Everything is energy, and the universe is constantly in motion. It doesn't care what you want. It doesn't pause for your hesitation. But you, you can move mountains the moment you decide to care. The moment you start moving.

You carry an entire universe inside of you. Remember?

You began as chemistry. A spark between two people. Then you became DNA, then cells. Then an embryo, a baby, a child, a teenager, an adult. And even now, you are still growing, changing, expanding. At every stage, atoms rearranged themselves to make you possible. You are a moving constellation of cells, water, and electricity. A living system. A biological miracle with a soul. You are proof that motion is sacred.

Sometimes, I simply go outside and walk. No plan, no destination, just air, space, and the rhythm of my feet against the pavement. It has carried me through more moments than I can name. Even at my lowest, when I have felt numb, unanchored, or entirely disconnected, I would lace up my shoes, pull on a hoodie, leave my phone behind, and go. Not to escape, but to return to myself. Walking reconnects me to rhythm, the rhythm of breath, of movement, of being alive.

I've walked in the cold, in the rain, in anger, in silence. I've walked until my breath softened and my thoughts began to shift. It's as if motion tricked my mind into remembering I'm still here, still breathing, still part of something. I stopped expecting instant transformation and started valuing the small shifts, a hello to a stranger, the way a building catches light, the sound of leaves under my feet. That's when the heaviness lifts, when I stop trying to arrive and simply allow myself to be in motion. Walking became my way of remembering myself. I didn't need a destination. It was never about being somewhere. It was about being here. So when things feel stuck, when my head gets too loud, I move. It doesn't solve everything, but it always changes something.

Working out is not a punishment. It's not a post-binge eating activity. It's literally just maintenance. You're in a body and it's all you've got; use it or lose it. And no, we're not doing this to be skinny. That's so dead. 1990s supermodels were not that skinny. I'm talking about the icons, not the cocaine-infused it-girls. They just had better photographers who knew the angles. Skinny is tired. Skinny is anxious. Skinny is cold and dizzy, and overthinking your life about whether you can eat the bread. Eat it. No one's going to die, and you're not going to gain a kilo. Muscles are the new skinny. Strong is hot. Strong is grounded. Strong is not texting your ex at 2 a.m. because you're too busy sleeping. You are tired. You worked your muscles out and pushed that weight. You are not interested in pillow talk. The phone is on silent and out of the room. Who cares if there is an emergency? You are so fit that you could climb down from your house to safety if you smelled the smoke.

It doesn't have to be sexy. It doesn't have to be aesthetic. Sometimes the workout is ugly. Sometimes you cry mid-squat. Sometimes your yoga pose resembles a piece of broken furniture someone abandoned on the side of the road. Who cares? You're not auditioning for the Olympics. You don't need to post your gym progression unless you're really just showing off your ass, in which case, that's cheeky and fully encouraged. You're trying to stay sane, sane in your body, sane in this world. And no, you're not weak because you're out of breath. You're out of breath because you've been avoiding your own power. You've been sitting in your head, arguing with imaginary people, building unrealistic get-rich masterplans so you never have to work again, which, side note, is a scam. Work is fun when you love what you do. Meanwhile, your body is like, "Hey. I'm still here. Let's do something about it." You don't need a fancy gym. You don't need those overpriced leggings. Honestly, steal that guy's shorts. You're just sleeping together, who cares? It's not about how it looks. Just move. For your hormones. For your blood pressure. For your peace. Move because it is your right. Move because it is your ritual. Move before you explode on the next person who chews too loudly. Obviously, I'm talking about myself.

Your body will thank you. The same goes for food. Eat things that make you feel alive, real food, colorful food, food that didn't come with a toy or a brand deal. Not because you are trying to shrink, but because your brain deserves proper fuel and your gut is not a landfill. Walk past the processed aisle. You are too impatient to read the labels anyway, and half the time, the ingredients list reads like a novel you didn't ask to start. Buy a cucumber, some bread with ingredients you can pronounce, and hummus that doesn't come with a narrative. Hummus should have no more than three ingredients. It is not a lifestyle brand. This is about self-respect. If your body is carrying you through life, the least you can do is carry it back. Most diets do not work because most diets were not made for women. They were made for men. In labs. With no hormonal chaos, no cravings, no PMS, no emotional breakdowns in Zara fitting rooms. Just straight-line biology and boring data. If you are a man reading this, let women know. Scream it from a rooftop and tell your sister to never skip her meals.

Stop starving yourself. Stop copying influencers. They don't even believe that shit they tell you. They tell you what the algorithm wants to push. Stop letting coffee raise your cortisol while you convince yourself you're "just not hungry in the mornings." You are. At least get yourself some organic protein or collagen and throw it in there. It's not cool to be dissociated and hungry in the morning. Eat food. Real food. Food with protein, color, and actual nutritional value. Not just bland crackers with a personality disorder. And please, for the love of blood sugar, stop switching diets every time someone with abs posts a "What I eat in a day." They don't even eat that. That's content. You're not content. You're a whole person. A human who goes to the toilet preferably once a day to let that shit go.

Find what works for you and stick with it long enough for your nervous system to stop thinking you are in danger. Once your body feels safe, it lets go. Of the weight, the drama, the inflammation, the bloating, the sudden urge to cry or start a fight over nothing. The goal is not perfection. The goal is ease. Strength, nourishment, and peace. The real power is in staying in motion even when you are still. Feel your breath move through your chest, steady and present. Now go get yourself a snack. You have earned it.

The world needs more movement. Movement of bodies, of spirit, of thought, of courage. Movement that disrupts stagnation and reminds us we were never meant to stand still.

Chapter 22
Love Truly Is the Thing

What is love? I don't know. I look directly at my audience sometimes when I'm performing, and sometimes I see people cry. Not because they are sad, but because they are moved. The biggest compliment is received through energy. When my audience opens itself up to me. When I'm not the only one in the room going through the motions. Everybody feels the love.

Becoming independent in the music industry came with numerous sacrifices and hard work. Not only did we release an entire album, but we also embarked on a full tour. As much as it was a very humbling moment to realize how much responsibility an artist carries going on tour independently, I also, in the middle of that process, understood what loving your craft means. My husband and I ensured that everything was meticulously planned, that everyone received their payment on time, and that our partners and the venues were satisfied. Meanwhile, I continued to work intensely to promote my Album, Part 4: The Witch. It was a lot.

It took a lot of energy and effort to create awareness and reach for an artist who was formally signed to a label backed with money, network, and resources. Through it all, giving up was never an option. I stuck to my vision. It is possible for a female mixed-race artist who does not chain herself or her identity to one style, culture, or music genre to showcase her work in a professional, independent manner. I was very disappointed by the lack of support I received from former business partners, industry friends, and colleagues, of course, not disregarding the ones that fully and wholeheartedly did. When you are led by love, your disappointment turns into motivation, and your motivation, combined with discipline and an impeccable work ethic, transforms into results.

I dedicate this book to all the people who loved me for who I truly was. I don't care if we don't talk anymore. Love is beautiful, and I'm lucky to have gone through life feeling loved despite everything I've been through. As much as I felt the sadness, the grief, and the anger, I also felt the love. I'm obsessed with feeling it and giving it. Living it and letting myself be guided by it. Nothing has a stronger frequency. Nothing matters more. That feeling when you are infatuated with something or someone rules us. It's an all-welcoming emotion that brings us to our knees and fills our hearts with warmth. Energy is defined as the capacity to work or produce change.. Energy is what gets things moving or heated; it's as simple as that. It appears in various forms and constantly changes shape, but never truly disappears. That's the rule.

We exist because of it, yet somehow we treat love like an optional upgrade, as if it's something we have to subscribe to if we want to. Unfortunately, we can't function without it. We never could. I once saw a man cry while walking his child on a busy street in Berlin. The child had a little green backpack on and was trying hard to keep up with his dad, rushing ahead, repressed sobbing, but it was visible to anyone who walked past him. God knows what he was going through. I couldn't even tell if he was going to a funeral or coming from one. He looked young but wise. Dark eyes and a baseball cap were being used to hide his tears. No one stopped. I did. That's when I understood: love is the only thing that stops time. It stopped the moment I asked how I could help. I'm here. He declined and kept walking. Community teaches us how to love and care for one another, and that's why it's so important.

Even if my own family did not set the best example of a community, I still feel that longing every day. We need to look out for each other more and spread more unconditional love. Without it, we will soon grow distinct. Our ability to feel will eventually become extinct; all that will be left will be apps, filters, make-believe, and Bitcoin. When we take our eyes off our screens and feel that looming emptiness and void, because there is nothing there, what do we do then? We step inwards and convince ourselves that we don't need each other to survive. That we can do this alone, that we are fine, that we like who we are, and that we don't have to change, instead everybody around us has to step up and change? We avoid the thought of wanting or needing someone because it hurts too much to think about losing them. You might not lose them. You could love them, and they might love you back forever. Who knows?! Don't let a difficult childhood or family constellation make you bitter. We need others to find each other. We do. It's inevitable. Love will save us if we practice it correctly. And if you can't open your heart to others, at least work on opening your heart to the world. Give yourself love, compassion, and grace. It's not tacky. It's iconic and vital.

Here are some important rituals of love. Be concerned with nature. Ask how it works, such as the ocean, the winds, the trees, and the animals. Take an interest in the very things that nurture you. Look at your naked body in the mirror without flinching. Take it all in, all the glorious expressions of skin, bones, form, and soul. Give yourself a hug and say, I love you just the way you fucking are, my love. The mirror was created to make you see yourself, but do you see yourself?

Next time you listen to music, don't just listen to it; engage with it. Pick a song you really love, a piece of music that brings tears to your eyes because it's so good. Sing along to it like your life depends on it. Look at people who are not like you with love. Look them in the eyes and smile. Fall in love with your friend, not because they are a lover, but because they are a beautiful human being with a fantastic character. Not because they are perfect, but because they exist.

I remember the days when I couldn't feel love. The days I was broken, hurt, and alone, and full of rage. I wanted to scream at the world: Why am I here? I don't want to be here. Drinking, partying, self-harming, and self-sabotaging, all that to realize that I could not find purpose in disrespecting the gift of life. This cage I was building for myself, built out of grief, rage, and insecurity, was starting to reveal itself as a total illusion. None of it was real, and it didn't feel real anymore. Not being afraid to get help was the first step. You are never alone, and you never will be. We are all made out of cells and DNA. We carry our ancestors within us and create new life to merge with future generations. We want to be felt, heard, seen, and loved.

I've had the honor of watching great performances by great musicians through my job and throughout my life, but nothing touches me more than seeing someone with genuine talent playing music in the street. I once saw someone play music in the street, a violinist, an angel playing the melody my heart needed to feel at that very moment. And just when I thought I didn't belong to this world, she took me back, back to reality, where things are beautiful when we do them with love. It's like holding a stranger's hand on the plane when they start crying after takeoff. It's about giving yourself grace after realizing you've made a mistake. It's hanging out with a friend that makes you laugh - and laughs at you for being unable to laugh at yourself.

Love is not a performance. It's a state of mind.

The greatest thing you will ever learn is to love and to be loved in return. I'm grateful for this lesson and everything that follows, and I would appreciate your participation. You deserve it; love that feels easy and isn't tied to a specific situation. Self, Love, Romantic love, Platonic love, Parental love. It doesn't matter. It's all love. And sometimes, when I forget, I remember the brave individuals who play music in our streets. Specifically, that girl with her violin. She didn't care if people stopped or even looked. She was in love with her violin. That's enough.

Thank you for spending time with me. I hope you feel inspired. Next time we meet, let's compare notes.

The world needs more love.